INDIA'S
FOREIGN POLICY
SINCE 1971

INDIA'S FOREIGN POLICY SINCE 1971

Robert Bradnock

PUBLISHED IN NORTH AMERICA FOR

THE ROYAL INSTITUTE OF INTERNATIONAL AFFAIRS

COUNCIL ON FOREIGN RELATIONS PRESS
• NEW YORK •

Chatham House Papers

General Series Editor: William Wallace
Asia–Pacific Programme Director: Peter Ferdinand

The Royal Institute of International Affairs, at Chatham House in London, has provided an impartial forum for discussion and debate on current international issues for 70 years. Its resident research fellows, specialized information resources, and range of publications, conferences, and meetings span the fields of international politics, economics, and security. The Institute is independent of government.

Chatham House Papers are short monographs on current policy problems which have been commissioned by the RIIA. In preparing the papers, authors are advised by a study group of experts convened by the RIIA, and publication of a paper indicates that the Institute regards it as an authoritative contribution to the public debate. The Institute does not, however, hold opinions of its own; the views expressed in this publication are the responsibility of the author.

Library of Congress Cataloguing-in-Publication Data

Bradnock, Robert W.
   India's foreign policy since 1971 / by Robert W. Bradnock.
      p.   cm.—(Chatham House papers.)
   Includes bibliographic references.
   ISBN 0-87609-089-7 : $14.95
      1. India—Foreign relations—1947–1984. 2. India—Foreign relations—1984–   I. Royal Institute of International Affairs.
II. Title. III. Series. IV. Series: Chatham House papers
(unnumbered)
DS480.84.B67   1990
327.54'009'047—dc20
                                                        90–2343
                                                           CIP

90 91 92 93 94 95 96 PB 10 9 8 7 6 5 4 3 2 1

CONTENTS

To Roma

ACKNOWLEDGMENTS

This book could not have been written without the help of many people who gave very generously of their time to discuss, read and comment at various stages of my work.

The following helped greatly with the fieldwork in India and Sri Lanka: the late S. Amirthalingam, Gopi Arora, Robert Boggs, Nigel Broomfield, Pran Chopra, Tarun Das, Kumari Jayawardena, Duleep Kumar, S.D. Muni, N. Ram, Chandra Schaffter, G.B. Singh, Jasjit Singh, Kushwant Singh, S.K. Singh, David Sprake, Neelam Tiruchelvam, Mark Tully and A.P. Venkateshwaran. I am particularly indebted to C.P. Singh for his constant openness to discussion.

In the United States Walter Anderson, Richard Cronin, Francine Frankel, Selig Harrison, Stanley Hegginbotham, Alvin Rubinstein and Robert Young all gave me invaluable time and guidance to Indian-American relations.

In Britain a number of scholars contributed generously either through participating in a Chatham House seminar or through commenting on a draft manuscript, among them Brian Bridges, Graham Chapman, Peter Duncan, Ben Farmer, Peter Ferdinand, Cherry George, Salman Haider, Michael Lipton, Peter Lyon, James Manor, David Taylor and K. Subrahmanyam. I am particularly grateful to John Toye and Michael Lipton for giving me pre-publication access to their book on aid and development in India.

The research would not have been possible without the generous financial support of the Royal Institute of International Affairs, nor

Acknowledgments

without the encouragement and patience of its Director of Studies, William Wallace. I should also like to thank the Publications Department and Gabrielle Galligan, the Asia-Pacific programme assistant, for their work on the text. The responsibility for all the views expressed remains mine alone.

Finally, my thanks are especially due to my wife Roma for continuous practical help and support.

July 1990   R.W.B.

1
INTRODUCTION

1971 was a turning-point for South Asia and for India's role in the region. The 1960s had been India's most difficult and demoralizing decade: what Selig Harrison, the American political journalist, had termed in 1960 the 'dangerous decade' had by 1970 become the decade of failure. It had begun with deteriorating relations with China, culminating in a disastrous and humiliating war in 1962. Nehru's death on 26 May 1964 marked a vital break with the politics of the freedom struggle. Would India be able to find its footing anew?

The middle of the decade gave little sign of encouragement. The Third Five-Year Plan (1961–6) ended in three years of drought which resulted in catastrophic agricultural failure and virtual economic collapse. India's much-heralded Five-Year Planning programme was suspended, large-scale imports of food aid became vital to prevent widespread starvation, and a World Bank-enforced devaluation in 1966 set the seal on India's apparent political and economic failure. Economists wrote of 'the failure of planning', and unfavourable comparisons were repeatedly made with Mao's China. The 1965 wars with Pakistan had done little to restore India's battered morale, for they were widely seen in India and outside as producing at best a stalemate. Then, just when Lal Bahadur Shastri, Nehru's successor as prime minister, seemed to be establishing himself, he died, immediately after signing the peace treaty with Pakistan at Tashkent.

The struggle for the succession which followed was bitter, and

Indira Gandhi's eventual victory was by no means assured. Her election triumph in 1971 over opponents both within and outside the Congress Party was a decisive domestic turning-point. Externally, the break-up of Pakistan and the signing of the Indo-Soviet Treaty of Friendship began new phases in India's relations both with its immediate neighbours and with the wider world, establishing it as the unchallengeable power within the South Asian region and potentially a force to be reckoned with further afield.

Yet even though 1971 was a turning-point for India, the outlines of its foreign policy had already been well established. By virtue of its size, history and location India was widely seen as a leading actor in the post-colonial world. Nehru's commitment to non-alignment with either of the superpowers fashioned a distinctive philosophy for India's foreign policy. Nehru himself captured the world's eye, but there were many forces at work in India's post-Independence democracy which created the national support essential for his broad philosophy to remain influential through to the present day.

By the late 1970s India was already, in John Mellor's words, 'a rising middle power'.[1] Today, with a population of over 810 million, an average annual industrial growth rate between 1980 and 1989 of over 7%, a GDP in 1990 of more than $250 billion, and a democratic political system that has survived over forty years of independence, India commands international attention.

India's armed forces grew from 280,000 in 1949 to over 1.36 million in 1990. The country has a diversifying technological base which now includes indigenously produced satellite launchers and nuclear power stations, and a pace of growth which has resulted in an urban population nearly four times the size of the total population of the British Isles. All these developments give India today a status and importance within South Asia that its neighbours at least take as axiomatic. Does this also suggest that India is within reach of playing a major role on the world stage?

This study examines India's regional and international significance today and the forces which have shaped its developing foreign policy since 1971. While the philosophy of India's foreign policy has been formed by the ideology of non-alignment, its practice has also reflected an essentially pragmatic pursuit of national interests. Indeed, the ideology itself has gained wide support within India, in large measure because it has fitted so closely a broadly shared perception of India's national interest. The question of India's possible wider aspirations is considered in Chapter 2. Domestic political issues, rooted in the social and regional realities of India and of South Asia, and also in economic goals and objectives which the government of independent India has pursued since 1947, have been of central concern. These are examined in Chapters 3 and 4. Chapter 5 analyses the way in which these concerns have influenced India's often tense and difficult relations with its neighbours, especially Pakistan, Sri Lanka and China.

Non-alignment was one way in which India tried to limit the penetration of cold war politics into its region, but it did not prevent the superpowers from bringing their inescapable influence to bear in South Asia. At the same time India has played an active part in adjusting to the new international environment which has been taking shape in the post-colonial world. India's policy with respect to its former colonial ruler, the United Kingdom, to the superpowers and to the wider world, is assessed in Chapter 6. Finally, Chapter 7 estimates India's potential for development as a significant power in world politics.

2
INDIA: MORE THAN A REGIONAL POWER?

India and its region

After Independence in 1947 the first charge on India's foreign policy was the relationship with its immediate neighbours. This concern stemmed not only from geographical proximity but from the nature of South Asia's geopolitical history. One of South Asia's paradoxes lies in the fact that while it had never been governed as a unitary state or developed a clear national identity, yet socially, economically and politically the region was remarkably integrated. A number of South Asian core areas had been centres of cultural development and of political power over four millennia, but their boundaries had been constantly shifting. The British-imposed borders between Pakistan and India bore little relation to any of these core regions or to any previously significant boundaries.[1]

Thus Partition in 1947, through which Pakistan was created on the basis of Islamic identity, disrupted many of the economic, social and political ties which had until that point been vital features of the political geography of the subcontinent. Even Nepal and Ceylon, which had developed distinct political identities, were linked with the rest of South Asia by common peoples, religions and cultures, as well as by economic ties.

The interwoven complexity of South Asia's political inheritance is illustrated by many of India's 550-odd pre-Independence princely states. The majority of these had predominantly Hindu populations governed by Hindu rajas. There were, however, a number of exceptions. Hyderabad and Kashmir, two of the most important,

4

provided immediate tests for the viability of the newly independent nation states of India and Pakistan. The Muslim Nizam of Hyderabad ruled a territory one and a half times the size of England and Wales, with a predominantly Hindu population. Kashmir's Hindu ruler governed a people over ninety per cent of whom were Muslim. The accession of Hyderabad to the Indian union was ensured by Home Minister Sardar Patel's so-called 'police action' of 1949, but Kashmir's relationship to India and Pakistan has remained the most bitterly divisive issue between the two countries.

The extent of cultural interaction between India and its immediate neighbours has contributed to the difficulty of developing new national identities, valid in themselves and unthreatening to one another. The 'two-nation theory' on which Muslim leaders had posited the creation of Pakistan was always rejected by Indian political leaders, and that rejection led many in Pakistan to believe that India was determined to undermine their country's independent viability. Many Pakistanis argued that India was openly unreconciled to the very concept of Pakistan for years after Independence. A.H. Syed writes, for example, that 'the reason for Pakistan's participation in military pacts with the West was dictated ... by the instinct for survival and self-preservation, in particular against possible Indian action aimed at undoing the partition'. As late as 1966 Z.A. Bhutto argued in the National Assembly that 'in the destruction of Pakistan lay India's most sublime and finest dreams' and, according to D.C. Jha, the then President Ayub Khan said that 'the leaders of India have not yet reconciled themselves to the very existence of Pakistan'.

A. Appadorai and M.S. Rajan argue an opposing view:

India's policy towards Pakistan, and in particular on the Kashmir issue, has in effect been determined by the secular character of the Indian state. Partition was advocated and accepted by Pakistani leaders on the basis of a two-nation theory, i.e. the Hindus and Muslims were two 'nations' and, therefore, should have their separate homelands. Indian leaders, while accepting partition sincerely, never approved of the two-nation theory. They accepted partition on the basis of some kind of territorial self-determination.[2]

One of the major developments within India since 1971 has been the strengthening of the government's public recognition of Pakistan's right to sovereign independence, but Pakistan's fear of Indian intentions remains a potent force. P.V. Narasimha Rao, addressing the Pakistan Institute of International Affairs on 11 June 1981 as Mrs Gandhi's foreign minister, argued:

> India should at least be credited with the perspicacity to know that there is not a single problem of hers which will come anywhere near solution by the undoing of Pakistan ... We on our part are convinced that we have an abiding interest, even a vested interest, in the stability of Pakistan ... I would like to state categorically, on behalf of the Indian people and India's Prime Minister, that India has, and will always continue to have, full respect for the sovereignty, territorial integrity, stability and independence of Pakistan.

Pakistan has never been the sole object of India's concern. India has genuine and significant interests in developments which take place in Nepal, Bangladesh and Sri Lanka. The exodus of 160,000 Tamil refugees into India from Sri Lanka in 1984, the flight of 50,000 Chakma tribal refugees from Bangladesh and the problems associated with Indian citizens of Nepali origin could not be wished away. Indeed, the movement of ten million refugees from East Pakistan into India in 1971 was a precipitating factor in the direct intervention by India which achieved the creation of Bangladesh.

Yet this very interweaving of the region's interests enhances its neighbours' fears that, despite protestations of disinterested non-interference, India will always find strict detachment difficult. How is the interlocking nature of India's interests with those of its neighbours reflected in its regional role?

India is by far the largest nation state in South Asia, and since the break-up of Pakistan in 1971 has been indisputably the major regional power. Figure 2.1 shows that India's GDP dwarfs that of its neighbours. While its industrial growth since 1965 does not compare with that of Korea or even China (see Figure 2.2), between 1980 and 1988 it was well in excess of that in OECD countries such as France and the United Kingdom.

The scale of industrial change and the evidence of India's growing military strength and diplomatic activity have prompted some Western observers to argue that India under Rajiv Gandhi was

Figure 2.1 Comparative GDP in 1965 and 1986

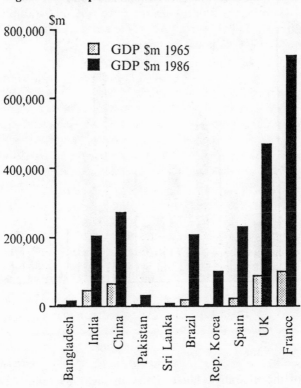

embarked on a strategy aimed at establishing regional dominance. Some would even see India as having ambitions to superpower status. Nicholas Ashford, a commentator on international relations in the British press, described India's relations with Nepal in 1989 as 'diplomatic bullying'. He argued that India's intervention in Sri Lanka and the Maldives, its military manoeuvres on the Pakistan border, and what he termed its 'support for rebels in Bangladesh's Chittagong Hills' were all evidence of this strategy by Rajiv Gandhi to dominate South Asia and the Indian Ocean.[3] Some trace that ambition back to Nehru himself.

Certainly voices have been raised in India demanding that the country take a place in the world commensurate with its potential strength. Such demands figured, for example, in the political plat-

Figure 2.2 Industrial growth 1965 and 1986 (%)

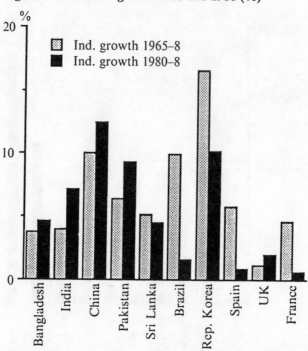

form of the Bharatiya Janata Party in the 1989 general election campaign which saw it win 88 seats in parliament: demands which were often couched in the language of resurgent Hindu chauvinism. But that was far from the goal of Nehru himself. It was his pursuit of economic development and global peace through non-alignment with either of the superpowers that gave India's foreign policy a high international profile.

American political scientists Robert Hardgrave and S.A. Kochanek argue that India aspires to be 'at least regarded as China's equal in world affairs'. They also suggest that 'domestic concerns impose constraints on India's role in the world, and India today is reluctant, as Nehru was not, to venture outside South Asia as a world actor'.[4] Whether or not that view is accepted, the evidence strongly suggests that India's foreign policy has been motivated by more mundane considerations than that of a chase for global superpower status. India was determined that its struggle for independence from Britain should leave it free not only in name but in practice. Under Nehru it set itself three essential tasks.

First, it had to build a full and permanent sense of national integration, as well as a fully democratic political structure, on the basis of the unprecedented degree of political unity achieved through the movement for independence.

Second, India was committed to achieving the largest possible measure of freedom of political action, in the international as well as in the domestic sphere. As Professor Leo Rose observed:

Nehru first proposed the total isolation of India and the rest of Asia from the western dominated world economy, and the construction of a self-reliant interdependent Asian economic system. He soon recognised that this was not feasible ... but his deep suspicions of the political impact of economic interactions with the western capitalist states became an integral aspect of his nonalignment policy.[5]

Nehru and other Indian leaders saw rapid economic progress as essential to realizing independence. India wanted to maximize its freedom to act internationally, unfettered by any constraints other than those of international law.

To achieve that freedom India set itself the third task, that of defending its own territory and its security interests, where necessary by developing armed services to meet any potential military threat.

The growth of India's military power: external security

India's military power has grown dramatically since Independence in 1947. Yet during much of the 1980s its security was still often seen within the country as remaining at risk. Certainly its military involvement in the break-up of Pakistan went some way to erasing the humiliating military defeat India had suffered at the hands of China nine years earlier. It also changed the geopolitical balance on the subcontinent. During much of the 1970s it seemed as if a new and constructive relationship between India and Pakistan could be achieved. However, the 1977 military coup in Pakistan and the Soviet occupation of Afghanistan in December 1979 brought prospects for an Indo-Pakistani entente to a juddering halt.

After the coup which brought him to power General Zia was viewed in the United States and the West with deep distrust. That distrust was transformed by the movement of Soviet troops across the Afghan border in 1979 into the belief that he represented the last bastion against Soviet expansionist ambitions in South Asia, and he obtained major American support for Pakistan in the 1980s. But India saw the rearmament of Pakistan as a direct challenge to its own security. The close ties between Pakistan and a Chinese government still strongly hostile to India only served to increase India's wariness about its external security position. In its view, that caution was vindicated by continued Chinese support for secessionist movements in India's North-East throughout much of the 1970s.

Figure 2.3 Military expenditure as % GDP, 1978–85

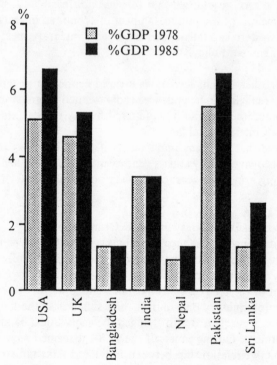

The increase in military spending in South Asia between 1978 (immediately before the Soviet occupation of Afghanistan) and 1985

appears more striking in absolute terms than when expressed as a proportion of GDP. It can be seen from Figure 2.3 that the proportion of GDP spent by Pakistan on the military, already higher than that of India, increased still further to 7%, while India's remained constant at just under 4%. Translated into absolute terms, however, military expenditure in India dwarfed that of its neighbours, and increased rapidly – to $9 billion – as GDP itself grew.

The volume of military spending in India's region has been only part of the story. Quality has been often been as important as quantity in terms of the region's international relations. China's nuclear capacity, the supply of F-16s and advanced AWACS radar equipment, which increased the sophistication of the Pakistani armoury, and the imminence of Pakistan's nuclear capability also stimulated India's burgeoning defence budget.

Internal security: fostering national identity
While external challenges to India's security had to be faced, India has also had to tackle the enormous task of strengthening national integration. In 1947 cultural and regional identities were often far stronger than the sense of Indian national identity, and welding together the diverse regions of India into one political unit for the first time in its history was bound to be profoundly complex. Politicians of a wide range of persuasions have often failed to rise to the challenge.

Religious identity has proved particularly problematic. The creation of Pakistan on the basis of its Islamic faith raised in sharp relief the question of the political status of India's many different religious communities. Even at Partition in 1947, 40 million Muslims remained in India. That number may have reached 100 million today. Secularism, enshrined in India's constitution, and the guaranteeing of rights to all religious communities to practise their beliefs and social customs, were an essential precondition of their acceptance of a unitary state. In the rhetoric of much political debate since 1947 the ideology of secularism has remained strong. However, while it is only the Hindu chauvinists of the right-wing Bharatiya Janata Party and their allies who demand a Hindu state, leaders of the Congress as well as of other political parties have observed the claims of secularism more in the breach than in the observance when it has suited them. And yet, as V.P. Singh's remarkable decision in November 1989 to appoint a Muslim to the highly sensitive post of Home Minister suggested, there remains a cross-party recognition that the secular constitution is the vital cement which binds the Indian union together.

After 1971 movements for greater regional political autonomy, notably in Punjab and in Assam, created continuing uncertainty. India's subcontinental diversity – of culture, language, ethnicity and religion – contains the seeds both of great strength and of challenge. In the domestic context that diversity has at times been used by political leaders to strengthen support for their parties. Mark Tully has documented the use made of Sikh extremists by Mrs Gandhi and the Congress Party to try to divide the Akali Party's opposition to Congress rule in Punjab as just one example of this process.[6] The survival of India's democratic constitution, interrupted only for the two years of Mrs Gandhi's emergency rule between 1975 and 1977, has thus far shown the flexibility and the strength to allow that diversity to be expressed within limits which sustain the overall fabric of national identity. However, as the communal violence that scarred the 1989 general election campaign in some states, notably Bihar, demonstrated, the tensions have often stretched India's political resources to the limit.

To some observers, India's very diversity severely inhibits the emergence of a coherent national identity. It lacks the rallying cry of fundamentalist religious belief that exists in some Islamic countries. Nor does it have the cultural unity bestowed by a predominant language and universally shared history, as in China. Without such strengths, India, it is argued, with its predominantly Hindu population but with a secular constitution designed to give equal rights to divergent minorities, cannot summon up the nationalist vigour to become a force in the wider world. Rather it will remain locked in introspection, struggling with its own political identity and viability.

At any rate the task of building the sense of national identity, though it has progressed a long way, is far from complete. It is a task that has had profound implications for the thrust of India's foreign policy.

The domestic economic challenge
India's continuing political and economic problems, many of which catch the attention far more than do its achievements, add to the

ambiguity over the extent of its role in world affairs. Sheer numbers make India the world's second largest country, with a population eight times greater than its neighbours Pakistan or Bangladesh. But those same numbers, still growing at a rate of about 2% a year, imply great economic, social and ecological costs. Thus since 1980, as Figure 2.4 shows, India's GDP has grown at more than twice the annual rate experienced in the United Kingdom,[7] and agricultural output has kept just ahead of population. Yet millions more of India's people were malnourished when Rajiv Gandhi left office than when his grandfather took up the prime ministership in August 1947.

Figure 2.4 Comparative growth GDP 1965–86 (% p.a.)

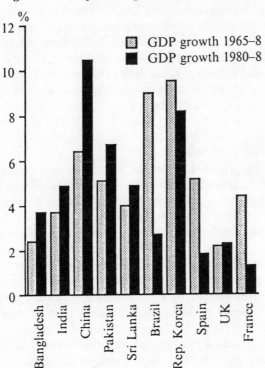

Of the 210 million or so people living in India's cities,[8] as many as seventy million live in the squalor of bustees, jhuggies and cheris – the squatter settlements which can be found right across India's urban landscape. At the same time, while rates of GDP growth and India's developing technological base may seem impressive, its performance in a wide range of fields has strong domestic critics. Thus C.N.R. Rao, Chairman of the Science Advisory Council to the prime minister, argued in August 1988: 'It is disheartening to admit that despite the tremendous infrastructure, we have only some islets of excellence in a sea of mediocrity. The quality of those coming for research sciences is poor. Our technological innovations and capabilities have just not grown.'[9]

That judgment may be over-pessimistic. At the same time, the pressures to achieve rapid economic progress encouraged Mrs Gandhi to re-examine some of her father's and her own Fabian principles of government economic control which had been central to the early years of Indian independence. The initial steps towards liberalization that she took in the early 1980s were strengthened after her death by her son Rajiv, who showed far greater sympathy for a free market economy. These policy changes had fundamental implications for India's economic relations with the rest of the world, which are explored in Chapter 4.

India and Indians in the wider world
India sought to protect its interests within its own region with vigour, but it also played a leading role in international forums such as the United Nations, the Commonwealth and the Non-Aligned Movement. It enhanced its already strong ties with the Islamic countries of the Middle East while at the same time becoming the Soviet Union's strongest and most important friend and trading partner in the developing world.[10] These developments all reflected a pragmatic response to India's perceived national interest, seen in terms of strengthening security and speeding up economic progress.

Such developments in India's international relations mark an obvious departure from the colonial legacy of close ties to the United Kingdom. As Lipton and Firn remarked in the mid-1970s, a pronounced change in the links with Britain was inevitable. They argued that a mature relationship 'cannot be built on blurred memories of a colonial relationship that did so little to solve India's key problems of this century – population, cereal farming, urban slums, industrial development ... the post-Colonial link has to rest on joint interests, not ex-Colonial sentiment.'[11]

Colonial political power, which had been brought to a *de facto* end when the Indian army marched into Goa on 17 December 1961, was given its last rites when India and Portugal restored diplomatic relations under a treaty signed on 31 December 1974.[12] This did not mean that India's colonial past was an unimportant influence on foreign policy, as the continuing strength of its economic ties with the United Kingdom in 1971 testifies. Almost half of India's foreign-owned capital in 1970 was British, a figure that remained as high as 47% in 1985.[13] At the same time India diversified its economic links with the rest of the world. As the relative share of the United Kingdom's trade with India has fallen from over 60% at Independence to around 7% now, that of other OECD countries, including the United States, has risen. In the mid-1980s, if oil imports from India's Bombay High were included, the United States was India's most important export market as well as being an increasingly important supplier of high-technology expertise and goods.

In addition to its close economic ties with the United Kingdom, a further distinctive legacy India inherited from the colonial period was the wide scatter of people of Indian origin across the world. Estimates of numbers vary widely.[14] Even figures for those living in the United States vary from 32,000 to over 600,000.[15] Despite the uncertainty over precise figures, both the scale and the geographical scatter of Indian emigration has been striking. Lemon and Pollock estimate that in the early 1960s there were over a quarter of a million settlers of Indian origin in South Africa, Mauritius, Burma, Fiji, the United Kingdom, Malaysia, Guyana and Trinidad, as well as smaller numbers elsewhere.[16] These figures exclude the million or so tea plantation workers of Indian origin in Sri Lanka. Apart from these, settlers of Indian origin abroad had a relatively slight and sometimes equivocal influence on India's foreign policy, as is demonstrated in Chapter 5. Yet important issues do continue to surround them – issues with which India often feels concerned. General Rambuka's coup in Fiji, support for Sikh nationalism in Britain, Canada and the United States, and the political and economic conditions of the three-quarters of a million Indians in South Africa all posed special problems for India's diplomacy.

Heimsath and Mansingh demonstrated that during the 1950s India's policy was self-contradictory: 'With respect to those overseas Indians who were foreign nationals – the bulk of them were in that category – it acknowledged the legal jurisdiction of foreign states and their responsibility for the settlers. But it simultaneously intervened diplomatically in order to improve their legal status, as Nehru candidly acknowledged in 1957.'[17]

Non-alignment and the Panchsheel
In his first broadcast to the nation on 7 September 1946, Nehru declared: 'We propose, as far as possible, to keep away from the power politics of groups, aligned against one another, which have led in the past to world wars and which may again lead to disasters on an even vaster scale.' But India's unwillingness to identify itself unequivocally with either superpower has strengthened the view of those who hold that it is a country fundamentally weakened by its inability to make up its mind. John Foster Dulles, writing in 1956, characterized India's non-aligned stance as 'obsolete, immoral and shortsighted', and despite the brief warming of relations during the Kennedy administration, which reflected in part American support for India during the war with China, successive US administrations have found non-alignment a difficult concept with which to come to terms.[18]

To Nehru, India's foreign policy had to reflect the complexity of the country's own domestic interests and the maintenance of its security. Nehru's commitment to the principles of non-alignment and international cooperation has to be seen in this light. Although Mahatma Gandhi had preached non-violence, it is quite wrong to suggest, as Nicholas Ashford does, that the Indian government had always paid lip-service to non-violence. Gandhi's views of non-violent resistance have never been the basis for the Indian government's foreign and security policy, though India has always stressed the importance of international cooperation and of acting through bodies such as the United Nations. Nehru argued that protection of India's interests, by force if necessary, was the first charge on foreign policy, though to the outside world it was the rhetoric of peaceful coexistence and mutual respect that caught the headlines.[19] K. Subramanyam, a former foreign policy adviser and leading analyst, has stressed that nonalignment 'was not merely a moral stand. As Nehru himself explained to Parliament, it was, in fact, also based on considerations of India's national interest.'[20]

But how far was India's foreign policy really in the hands of Nehru alone? Nehru took a modest view of his own role,[21] but many would share Roy Jenkins's opinion that Nehru 'gave India in the 1950s a major presence in the world scene – a presence greater than, even with its somewhat more solid economy, it has today.'[22] This point was made even more forcibly by one of Nehru's early biographers, Michael Brecher: 'Nehru is the philosopher, the architect, the engineer and the voice of his country's policy towards the outside world.'[23] The British journalist and writer Geoffrey Moorhouse argued that 'Nehru gave India a place on the world stage through sheer force of personality.'[24]

But did non-alignment survive Nehru in rhetoric only? Was the Indo-Soviet Treaty of Friendship, signed in 1971, its death certificate? Certainly the Janata government's election in 1977 was accompanied by Morarji Desai's promise to return to 'genuine non-alignment', though at the end of nearly three years of government the economic and military ties with the Soviet Union were stronger than ever. But, as is shown below, there are grounds on which India's stance can still be justified as non-aligned, a stance reiterated with force by the government of V.P. Singh, elected in November 1989.

Through the forty years of independence India's foreign policy has retained a fundamental consistency of strategic outline which has survived both changes of personal leadership and changes of government. Nehru's 'Panchsheel', or five principles,[25] are still held up as the basis of India's foreign policy today: mutual respect for territorial integrity and sovereignty, mutual non-aggression, mutual non-interference in internal affairs, equality and mutual benefit, and peaceful coexistence.

Such principles scarcely read like a manifesto for the attainment of world power status. Critics of India's foreign policy in action suggest that their repetition today, three and a half decades after their adoption at the Bandung Conference, is sanctimonious hypocrisy. Such critics point to the extent of India's direct involvement in its neighbours' affairs and to its willingness to resort to force in protection of its own vital interests.[26] Indian governments reply that they have taken an active part in neighbours' internal affairs only at the direct invitation of their governments, or, in the case of the 1971 war with Pakistan, when India's own territory was attacked. But India has never concealed its determination to protect its national interest, and it has not hesitated to apply pressure on its neighbours to secure its policy objectives.

Nehru saw non-alignment between the superpowers at the time of the cold war as a vital precondition to protecting that national interest. In the words of Professor Raju Thomas, he argued that 'greater security could be achieved through non-involvement in military blocs' than through being tied to one or other side in the cold war. Non-alignment was a pragmatic as well as an idealistic stance, and as Thomas argues, 'the practice of non-alignment ... suggests a flexible standard to be adapted to the prevailing strategic circumstances'.[27]

So can India's foreign policy be understood in terms of Nehru's high-profile principles? Against the constantly shifting backcloth of the international and domestic situation, how have Nehru's foreign policy principles been translated into practice? The broad framework of India's foreign policy has shown a remarkable degree of consistency. But by its nature foreign policy is often expressed as a reaction to external events. India's foreign policy has been no exception, and few of India's major actions in the field of foreign affairs since 1971 have resulted from long-term strategic planning.

Professor Robert Hardgrave, an American political scientist, suggested in 1984 that 'decision-making in Indian foreign policy tends to be informal, ad hoc, and reactive. It involves no grand design or long range strategy but a framework for tactical manoeuvres.'[28] From the early confrontation with Pakistan over Kashmir, through the war with China in 1962, the 1965 and 1971 wars with Pakistan, and more recently the intervention in Sri Lanka, India's action has been responsive rather than creative. K. Subramanyam writes of the structure of decision-making in the prelude to the 1962 clash with China: 'What struck me was the absence of an integrated view of international developments at various levels of government in spite of Prime Minister Nehru's own uncluttered perception of them.'[29] In some key respects it may be argued that little seems to have changed, and Litwak has argued with respect to the developments of India's armed forces during the 1970s: 'A detailed analysis of the arms purchases would reveal that, as and when a major acquisition of weaponry by Pakistan was foreseen, India reacted to it quickly and adequately by resorting to import of weapons.'[30]

India's geopolitical realities
Although reaction to events rather than long-term planning has

remained a feature of Indian foreign policy-making, this is not to say that there has been no strategic thinking or planned foreign policy. Far from it. The more important of these detailed policy developments are discussed in subsequent chapters. Alongside the short-term and the immediate there has remained a consistent thread of pragmatism running through India's foreign relations.

To understand this consistency it is necessary to appreciate India's geopolitical position in Asia. In 1947 India had over 15,000 km of land border, shared mainly with Pakistan and China. By 1971 India and Pakistan had fought three wars. Although the creation of Bangladesh from what had been East Pakistan produced a major change in India's geostrategic position with respect to its neighbours, the relationship with Pakistan remained its overwhelming security consideration.

Pakistan's geographical contiguity with Islamic states to the west and its natural and persistent efforts to strengthen the political coherence of Islamic identity in the region were one influence on India's efforts to develop and sustain the best possible relations with the states of West Asia.[31] This objective was further supported by the continued Muslim presence in India after Partition, and after the oil crises of the 1970s an economic incentive was also added. From 1962 India's external security situation worsened sharply, with its defeat at the hands of China and the development through the 1960s of links between China and Pakistan. Non-alignment still seemed to offer the best prospects for keeping superpower conflict out of the South Asian region, but it was a difficult policy to sustain in the face of a cold war confrontation in which countries across the world were being constantly pressured to choose sides.

For one thing, China and the Soviet Union are by the nature of Asian geography far more immediately significant for India's security than are the United States or Western Europe. Indeed, in a backhanded way the point is made by Zbigniew Brzezinski when he presents a map of the world as seen from Washington: India is dropped off each side. This is a point to which we shall return in Chapter 6 when considering Indo-US relations.[32]

Under Stalin the Soviet Union itself saw little interest in developing strong links with the 'bourgeois India',[33] but from 1954, under Khrushchev's guidance, that perception began to change. One reason for the changing Soviet view of India was the decision of the United States to supply arms to Pakistan, and Western support generally for Pakistan's position on Kashmir in the United Nations. Together, these created a new set of perceptions in India as to its international interests, opening the door to overtures from the Soviet Union. The visit of Bulganin and Khrushchev in late 1955 was the first positive step down the path to today's mutual friendship.

By 1968 the Soviet Union had already decided that India could play a vital role in its Asian security policy, and the coincidence of interests with India's own security concerns was cemented by the formation of a Chinese-Pakistani axis and by the Nixon-Kissinger initiative towards China. The signing of the Indo-Soviet Treaty of Peace and Friendship in 1971 was a joint recognition of the strength of mutual interest that bound them.

Those common interests and the closeness of the relationship that developed have often been misinterpreted, particularly after the Soviet occupation of Afghanistan. To some the Indo-Soviet Treaty signalled the end of non-alignment. Chawla argued in 1975 that by accepting American help 'for all practical purposes India's non-alignment posture was meaningless after 1962',[34] but it was commonly held in the United States and elsewhere in the West that India passively toed the Soviet line after the signing of the treaty. Certainly, as Rose has pointed out, the treaty 'included a consultation clause that Nehru himself would have considered a violation of the basic principles of non-alignment'.[35]

Yet India retained its independence of action in all the areas where its interests differed from those of the Soviet Union. Despite an initially muted reaction, Mrs Gandhi soon made clear after her return to power in 1980 that the Soviet occupation of Afghanistan was very much against India's long-term interests, and she repeatedly argued the case for withdrawal with both Brezhnev and Gromyko. But that did not change the fact that India also had very strong interests in common with the Soviet Union. As Litwak argued in 1984: 'Indian foreign policy decision-making is explicable in terms of the broad bounds of Indian national interests ... It is hard to envisage the development of any form of intensified relationship between the Soviet Union and India in which the former could compel the latter to act against its wishes.'[36]

Thus India resisted all Brezhnev's urging to join an Asian security pact, a proposal which India saw as an unwelcome invitation to gang up on China. Likewise it avoided giving any support to

Gorbachev's Vladivostok proposal to convene a conference on security in Asia and the Pacific. It dismissed suggestions that India might provide naval facilities for the Soviet fleet. Perhaps it is testimony to the Soviet Union's recognition that such a request would be totally unacceptable that it was hardly pressed.

The reactive nature of key Indian foreign policy decisions has to be seen in the context of a broadly consistent philosophy, shared by successive governments. Does that consistency of philosophy reflect the close integration of foreign policy with the constraints of serving domestic security objectives, as Nehru was arguing? Or does it actually reflect the nature and interests of a foreign policy-making elite exercising power virtually autonomously, above India's domestic political concerns? And even where such concerns were a prime motivating force behind foreign policy, has that policy always been developed on the basis of the cool reason and the national interest with which Nehru appeared to justify it? These questions are considered in the next chapter.

3

THE DOMESTIC ROOTS OF INDIA'S FOREIGN POLICY

Nehru argued that 'external affairs will follow internal affairs'. India's domestic polity certainly had a profound influence on its relationships with its neighbours and with the outside world. Despite the break-up of Pakistan and the signing of the Indo-Soviet Treaty of Peace and Friendship in 1971, India still continued to experience the political tensions and economic challenges which had been overriding concerns for the government at Independence. To the outside world India seemed firmly established in South Asia's driving seat, but its foreign policy demonstrated continuing anxiety over its regional security. This anxiety reflected not only events within South Asia and beyond, but also its own struggle to weld diversity into political strength and to replace poverty with prosperity.

Since 1971 India has experienced severe problems with three of its closest neighbours, Pakistan, China and Sri Lanka, and periodically poor relations with Bangladesh and Nepal. For a country that has consistently claimed to adhere to principles of peaceful coexistence and mutual non-interference in the affairs of foreign countries, it may appear an undistinguished record.

Yet to Indian eyes the threats to its security have been all too real. Ever since 1947 Pakistan has loomed like a threatening shadow to the north-west. It continues to exercise the greatest hold on the Indian government's attention. The much-quoted dictum of Kautilya, the Indian statesman and strategist of the fourth century

BC, that 'the enemy of my enemy is my friend' may appear to have been a guiding principle for contemporary Indian foreign policy, India's friendships with Afghanistan and the Soviet Union being seen as counterweights to the hostility of Pakistan and China. But the roots of India's foreign policy towards its neighbours go deeper than that strategic doctrine might suggest.

One part of India's colonial inheritance was a record of ninety years' systematic exploitation of the internal divisions of South Asia as a tool for sustaining imperial power. Professor Wayne Wilcox, writing with respect to the relationship between the Indian princes and the British, put the point with force. He argued that after the Mutiny of 1857, the British

> ... lavishly acknowledged their debt to the princes. A policy of support for the division of India was enshrined in imperial dogma for ninety years, the full span of British rule, and notions of indirect administration spread throughout the colonies. Another policy which was equally important in the future was the crushing of the Muslims of India.[1]

By 1971 these divisions still remained, providing opportunities for those hostile to India's development as a regional power to weaken its economic and political base. Both geography and history suggested the vital necessity of policies which could promote cohesion.

After 1971 the broad outlines of India's foreign policy remained largely those laid down by Nehru more than twenty years earlier. The extraordinary fact that India was under the political leadership of three generations of the Nehru family for all but five years since 1947 contributed to that continuity. But given the open nature of political activity and political debate in India through most of that period, it is necessary to look beyond the purely personal influence of Nehru himself, of his daughter Indira Gandhi and of his grandson Rajiv Gandhi, to understand why foreign policy sustained such a wide measure of political support within India long after Nehru's death.

To a great extent this support reflected the nature of India's internal social, political and economic framework, and a shared perception of the major external threats. Its continuance has been the result not so much of the autonomy of foreign policy-making, however much that has remained under the personal control of successive prime ministers, as of the degree to which in its broad outlines it has reflected a common view of India's regional and global interests. This chapter explores the relationship between those domestic influences and the development and practice of foreign policy.

A secular state? The party political base

At the heart of contemporary India's national viability lies its secular constitution. As Peter Lyon has argued, 'it was politically and psychologically important for Nehru, the arch anti-communalist, that the country whose Prime Minister he had become was named not Hindustan but India'.[2] In 1960 Selig Harrison expressed a view that had widespread currency in the following decade, arguing that India would have to fight incipient Balkanization. He identified caste, political parties, and language as potentially divisive forces. Both religion and regionalism were further sources of sharply contrasting and sometimes conflicting marks of identity.

The government of newly independent India was determined to give all groups freedom, not only of belief but also of practice according to that belief. Only through the apparent paradox of one of the world's most religious societies enshrining a secular basis to its constitution did Nehru, Gandhi and other leaders of the movement for independence see any prospect of developing a sense of identity with and loyalty towards India as a nation that would overarch the many other potentially divisive identities.

In practice the ideal of a secular state was frequently put under severe pressure by political parties (including the Congress Party) acting in response to religious, communal or linguistic interests. Ever since Independence, India's domestic political structure has been profoundly unbalanced. The Congress Party, having led the struggle for independence for over sixty years, was the only genuinely national party, covering the whole nation as an effective electoral force. Although other political parties such as the Muslim League or the South Indian Justice Party had established their own support bases, none had the universalist character of the Congress Party. Its strength lay not just in its successful pursuit of national independence but in its appeal to India's minorities, notably the lower-caste Hindu communities, Muslims and Christians. Through the powerful advocacy of Mahatma Gandhi it had championed the cause of the Harijans[3] or outcastes, and it legislated to reduce the barriers to the economic and social progress of the lower Hindu castes and other minorities by extending the measures of positive discrimination introduced before Independence. At the same time it tried to meet the latent and sometimes openly expressed fears of many Muslims that despite India's secular constitution Hinduism was the dominant social and political force. It is striking, for example, that India was the first country to ban Salman Rushdie's novel *Satanic Verses* out of deference to Islamic opinion.

In practice the Congress Party's ideological spectrum was extremely broad, ranging from Nehru's Fabian socialism through to populist nationalism, and it attracted the support of very diverse interest groups. The struggle for independence from Britain had bound these groups together. An effective party democracy and the decentralization of power within the party to elected representatives from all the regions provided mechanisms for the resolution of intra-party disputes, but Nehru's hold on foreign policy was unchallenged. It was actively supported both within the Congress Party and across party lines because it was justified in terms of pursuing a genuinely national interest.

Up to its defeat in the November 1989 general election the Congress Party was out of power in central government for less than three of independent India's forty years of democratic government. But that fact overstresses the party's popularity, for in most elections it received less than 45% of the national vote. India has a kaleidoscope of political parties at the national and regional level. Given the country's federal system, in which states elect their own legislative assemblies, the Congress Party has fought a wide range of different opponents across the country in both state and central government elections.

Although several of the parties described themselves as 'socialist' it is impossible to attach precise ideological labels to their diverse programmes. With the exception of the Communist Party of India (Marxist) in West Bengal and Kerala, most of the Congress Party's opponents at a regional level based their programmes on the appeal of ethnic populism. The Sikh-supported Akali Party in Punjab, the National Conference of Sheikh Abdullah and his son Farooq in Kashmir, the All India Anna Dravida Munnetra Kazhagam (AIADMK) and the DMK in Tamil Nadu, the Telugu Desam in Andhra Pradesh and the Shiv Sena in Maharashtra – all gained power through campaigning on local and regional populist issues. Political activity at the state level was a constantly shifting pattern of alliances and enmities, often regional and personal in character rather than national and ideological. Opposition to the Congress Party after 1971 came from across the ideological spectrum and from a wide range of regional and sectional interests. Nevertheless these interests were very largely concerned with domestic issues, and no consistently distinctive stance on foreign policy was taken by any of the non-Congress parties, even those with a strong ideological leaning.

The veteran Communist Party (Marxist) leader of West Bengal, Jyoti Basu, has been Chief Minister of the state since June 1977, during which time his opposition to the central government has been as strident and consistent as any. But in foreign policy issues the West Bengal government has often supported Congress actions. The most recent example came from Jyoti Basu's visit to Beijing in June 1988. He was reported as saying on his return: 'The Chinese leadership asked me whether Rajiv Gandhi is sincere and I said, of course. I told them that we differ from the Central Government on many subjects but on this we are together'.[4]

This consensus reflected the common view held by the state government of West Bengal and the central government in New Delhi over the domestic issue of the creation of a separate state for Gorkhas, and the fear in both quarters that the Chinese could provide backing for a movement that was perceived as against the interests of both.

The only real test of non-Congress attitudes to foreign policy before the 1989 general election was provided by the Janata government of 1977–9. The fierce resentment at Mrs Gandhi's two-year emergency rule between 1975 and 1977 encouraged the diverse parties opposed to the Congress to come together as the Janata ('People's') Party. Cobbled together within a period of two months, the Janata Party won an astonishing victory when Mrs Gandhi called an election in 1977. Crossing the ideological spectrum from the right-wing Hindu nationalist party, the Jana Sangh, through to left-wing parties like the Socialist Party, the Janata government promised at first to return to 'genuine non-alignment'. Morarji Desai, the first Janata Party prime minister, had sharply criticized the 'Soviet tilt' of Mrs Gandhi's previous government. In practice he and his foreign minister, A.B. Vajpayee, a leading figure in the earlier Jana Sangh Party, rapidly made clear that the foreign policy of the new government would differ little in essentials from that of its predecessor. Indeed, after nearly three years in power the Janata government had strengthened India's ties with the Soviet Union without gaining any of the promised improvement in relationships with the United States.

The general election in November 1989 was contested for the first time since 1977 by a concerted opposition to the Congress Party across the country. The National Front, which contained many of the constituents of the old Janata Party and regional parties like the DMK and the Telugu Desam, was able to reach agreement with the Bharatiya Janata Party and the Communist Party (Marxist) over seat allocations, thereby enabling a straight fight to take place in the great majority of constituencies. Its partial victory – the result left it well short of an absolute majority – resulted from an almost complete rejection of Rajiv Gandhi's government across northern India.

Throughout the campaign leaders of the National Front promised to improve relations with India's neighbours, to attempt more vigorously to improve relations with China and to reiterate India's non-aligned stance. Yet in real terms there is little to suggest that the major thrust of foreign policy is likely to alter any more than it did through changes of government in 1977 and 1979. A symbol of that continuity was graphically provided by Mrs Gandhi's decision to retain the Janata government's ambassador to the Soviet Union, I.K. Gujral, in Moscow. His appointment to the post of foreign minister by V.P. Singh in November 1989 suggested, moreover, that a strong element of continuity could be expected in the foreign policy of the current National Front government.

Threats to internal stability since 1971: regionalism, ethnicity and political identity

Minorities in themselves do not necessarily influence either domestic or foreign policies, but India's minorities have often had a political significance out of proportion to their numbers. It is impossible to understand the origins of India's permanently strained relationships with Pakistan, for example, or its difficulties in the late 1980s over Sri Lanka, without reference to the domestic interests of which foreign policy was a projection. The same may be said for the difficulties India and Bangladesh had over questions such as the sharing of the water of the Ganges at Farakka, Bangladeshi migrants in Assam or the Chakma refugees from the Chittagong hill tracts. Equally, the periodic tensions between India and Nepal, of which the disputes in spring and summer 1989 were only the latest examples, reflected not just Nepal's geostrategic significance for India but also the intimate links between domestic concerns like the Gorkhaland question and the status of people of Nepali origin living in India. Newspaper cuttings at the time seemed to suggest that the disagreements were new, but they have existed on and off ever since 1947, and are rooted in Nepal's deep sense of dependency and the permanent threat to its independent viability not just from India but also from China.[5]

Kashmir

Since 1971, a succession of political crises, with their origins in domestic concerns, posed problems for India's relations with its immediate neighbours. The most intractable of these problems has been that of Kashmir. For Pakistan, the fact that Kashmir has a Muslim majority population is justification enough for the state to have been conceded automatically to the Islamic state of Pakistan. The legal right of the rulers of princely states to accede to whichever nation they wished on Independence in 1947, pressed at the time by the Muslim League, is no longer deemed a relevant consideration. Yet for India, to concede the role of religious affiliation now as a deciding principle of national identity is seen as cutting the root of secularism. To say that the three million Muslims of Kashmir should be given a state simply because they are Muslims would immediately raise the question of the national status of the additional 100 million Muslims living elsewhere in India. Does their allegiance, too, really lie with Pakistan? It is a question to which Indian Muslims have repeatedly given a resounding 'no'. It is hardly surprising that the great majority of Muslims in India are strongly opposed to the transfer of Kashmir to Pakistan on those grounds.

In a truly dramatic gesture, V.P. Singh's first prime ministerial appointment after his election victory of 1989 was that of the first Muslim ever to hold the post of India's Home Minister. While the intention was to send an unequivocal signal to Muslims throughout India that the new government was fully committed to the maintenance of minority rights, the appointment was greeted in Kashmir by the immediate abduction of the new Home Minister's daughter by separatist extremists. In summer 1990 there was no sign that the police and military clampdown in Kashmir had brought a political solution within sight.

India's Muslim minority

Communal competition between South Asia's Hindu and Muslim populations was part of the colonial legacy. The Congress Party sought to neutralize that conflict and succeeded in gaining a large measure of popular support from the Muslim community. However, over the last fifteen years there has been a resurgence of communal conflict. Between 1978 and 1982 the number of communal incidents reported by the Ministry of Home Affairs rose from 230 to 474 and over 1,100 people were killed. By 1990 the numbers were still rising. In part this increase was the result, as Professor Paul Brass suggests, of the fact that 'pluralist policies, though not discarded, were often subordinated to short-range calculations of political benefit'.[6]

Indian sensitivity to the Muslim minority after 1947 encouraged India to develop and maintain strong links with the whole Islamic world. Such policies continued after 1971, whatever political upheavals took place within the Islamic world itself. Until the overthrow of the Shah's regime, for example, India made every effort to develop trade links with Iran, notably through exporting iron ore for the Shah's ambitious steel expansion programme. While in part this was to help pay the rapidly increasing oil bill resulting from the 1973 oil crisis, it was also designed to prevent the links between Iran and Pakistan from developing into a military alliance aimed at India. The overthrow of the Shah and the fundamentalist revolution in Iran did not inhibit India's efforts to maintain good relations with that country, though they proved far less successful than during the Shah's regime. At the same time India did everything possible not to take sides in the Iran-Iraq war. Indeed, oil imports from Iran and Iraq, which were minimal in 1978, grew equally fast in the following three years.

Other Islamic states also figured prominently in India's foreign policy. Saudi Arabia and the Gulf states used some of their surplus revenue in the 1970s and 1980s to support Islamic causes worldwide and directly strengthened economic and cultural links with Pakistan. At the same time Saudi Arabia welcomed Pakistani troops to assist in training its own forces. However, Saudi Arabia and other Gulf states also opened their doors to Indian labour. In India it was

largely the Muslim population that benefited from the new opportunities available in the Gulf, but they gave the Indian government an
important stake in the Middle East, in addition to the region's role
as India's chief supplier of oil. The Gulf became a growing market
for Indian goods and the base of operation for powerful non-
resident Indians. These new contacts strengthened Middle Eastern
countries' awareness of the political and economic importance of
India in the region.

Punjab

In Punjab, Tamil Nadu and Assam the domestic political battle-
ground again had far-reaching implications for foreign policy issues.
The demand for greater autonomy for the Sikhs threatened the
stability of the geostrategically vital borderland with Pakistan, and it
created disaffection among a minority group which played a vitally
strategic role in India's development and security. Not only was
Punjab agriculturally the most progressive and prosperous state, but
the Sikhs played a quite disproportionately important role, in
relation to their numbers, in the armed services. But the Sikh
community is also one of the most widely scattered outside India.
Small groups of Sikhs in Britain, Canada and the United States have
supported the movement for an independent Sikh state. Events such
as the detonation of a bomb on an Air India jumbo jet near Ireland
in 1986 internationalized the Punjab question.

Demands for an independent Sikh state strike at the heart of
India's secularism in what is, geographically, one of India's most
sensitive regions. Punjab shares a boundary with Pakistan, allowing
cross-frontier movement should Pakistan wish to permit or
encourage it. Sikh militancy thus puts yet another vital stretch of
sensitive territory at risk, extending India's border of insecurity from
the Aksai Chin and the Siachen glacier in the far north of Kashmir
right down to the desert wastes of Rajasthan and the Rann of
Kutch.

The journalist Khushwant Singh, writing in the *Indian Express* on
18 May 1987, identified the importance for India's wider interests of
not conceding the territorial demands made by Haryana in relation
to the Punjab Accord. 'Transfer of territories on basis of religion (or
language) militates against the spirit of secularism and national
integrity.' The influence of militant Sikh demands in Punjab had
already produced its counter in a revival of Hindu militancy in the

mid-1980s. In 1988 there were over a thousand terrorist killings (over half the number of deaths caused by acts of terrorism in the world as a whole). In the 1989 general election imprisoned Sikh militants won landslide victories in Punjab. V.P. Singh's decision to free the militants from jail and to visit the Golden Temple in Amritsar himself were Gandhian gestures of reconciliation, but the road to a permanent settlement still seems likely to be a bumpy one.

Tamil Nadu and Sri Lanka
The ethnic conflict in Sri Lanka raised a different problem for the Indian government with respect to Tamil Nadu. It is easy to overstate the strength of the ties between Sri Lankan Tamils from Jaffna and the 50 million Tamils living in Tamil Nadu. Although they do share a cultural tradition, more than 1,000 years of geographical separation had left the two communities with a somewhat distant friendship and often very little sense of common political interest. That was changed by the crisis in Sri Lanka in 1983 which caused 160,000 refugees to flee to South India.

Until 1983 India had dealt with Sri Lanka entirely on a government-to-government basis, engaging in little consultation with the state government of Tamil Nadu. The southern tip of Tamil Nadu is 2,500 kilometres from New Delhi, while the Pakistani border is only 500 kilometres from the capital. That great distance may have contributed to the limited awareness shown by Nehru and his government of the pressures of cultural and regional identity in the Tamil-speaking areas of South India in the first fifteen years after Independence. The electoral dominance of the Congress Party in South India during the first twenty years of independence and the powerful position within the Congress of Tamil leaders such as Kamaraj Nadar appeared to justify the view that demands for Tamil political autonomy were made only by an extremist minority.

By 1966, the issue of Hindi, which the government had intended should become the sole national language by that date, had helped to transform a Congress stronghold into a region of permanent regional party rule. The DMK led agitations throughout Tamil Nadu against the imposition of Hindi. As the date approached, widespread language riots broke out. The central government was forced to retract. However the damage to the Congress Party inflicted by the dispute was overwhelming. Arguably it was worsened by the Shastri government's agreement with Mrs

31

Bandaranaike's government in Sri Lanka (the 'Sirimo-Shastri Pact') to accept the repatriation of three-quarters of a million Tamil tea estate workers. In the 1967 elections to the State Assembly the Congress Party was routed, and thus a warning flag was hoisted, indicating that central government could neither ignore the political implications of strong regional identities nor take foreign policy decisions with India's neighbours without reference to regional interests.

It is ironical that the DMK's demands for a separate nation state had been dropped by its leader C.N. Annadurai only in 1962, as a direct result of India's war with China. That war roused Indian nationalist feelings across the country and support for separatism withered. The consolidation of the DMK's support for integration with India has survived both the party's split into two factions and the post-1983 crisis in Sri Lanka. The Congress government took advantage of the split in the old DMK by allying itself with the breakaway faction led by M.G. Ramachandran, the All India Anna DMK. After 1983 its concern about the political pressures from within Tamil Nadu were enhanced by the flood of Tamil refugees from Sri Lanka, imposing an economic burden and a potentially explosive political liability.

Assam and India's North-East

Vital domestic interests were also at stake in Assam from the late 1970s until the signing of Rajiv Gandhi's Accord in 1986. As a frontier where the potential and actual power of China and India confronted each other, Assam and the North-East had become a real security concern to the British after 1912. Nehru's belief that India and China could sustain a close friendship without compromising on the colonial boundaries was shattered by the 1962 war with China. After that defeat Assam had a magnetic strategic attraction, drawing it and the whole of the north-eastern region into the mainstream of Indian political action.

Mrs Gandhi was sufficiently concerned by Assamese Hindu claims of large-scale illegal immigration from Bangladesh to risk a significant worsening of India's relationship with that country by promising to build a guarded fence round the whole length of India's frontier. However unlikely the actual building of such a fence may have been,[7] Mrs Gandhi was willing to accept a poorer relationship with Bangladesh at a time when the dispute over the shared water of the Ganges at Farakka was still proving intractable. Both the hold of the Congress Party and the firmness of the north-eastern region's embrace in India came under tremendous strain at the end of the 1970s. Finding a solution to that domestic crisis was far more important strategically to the government than the possibility of short-term embarrassments with Bangladesh.

Fear of China's ability and willingness to use instability in Assam and the north-east frontier region as a wider destabilizing force contributed to the long period of cool silence between the Indian and Chinese governments throughout the 1970s and early 1980s. At the same time Assam played an important economic role for the rest of India as a major supplier of oil. The interruption of that supply forced India to import even more oil and chemicals than would otherwise have been necessary, causing a significant drain on India's foreign-exchange reserves.

The wider political stalemate between India and China made it impossible to resolve the major outstanding problem between them, the lack of an agreed demarcated boundary through the Himalayan frontier region. In itself the lack of clarity over the boundary caused no immediate problems, but it left open possibilities for dispute which its resolution would have made less likely. Thus the decision in 1986 to grant full statehood to Arunachal Pradesh, a decision taken by Rajiv Gandhi for internal domestic reasons, led the Chinese to believe that India might move on a wider front to assert claims to territory which in its own eyes was still disputed. They responded with military manoeuvres. There were no objective reasons for conflict between India and China in mid-1987 and it now seems that the scale of those manoeuvres was greatly overestimated, but Indian sensitivity about the region was demonstrated by the immediacy of the public concern as well as of the government's action in 1986.

After 1971 Assam was not alone in providing sharp reminders of the potential of ethnic and religious issues to fragment India's political unity. The Shiv Sena (a Maratha regionalist party) in Bombay, for example, made political capital out of the presence of immigrants to the city from southern India. As Weiner has shown,[8] when competition between groups develops on the basis of rising but unfulfilled economic expectations, national identity can readily be displaced by other more local identities.

In Assam the early objects of Assamese Hindu distrust were not

33

the Bengali Muslim agriculturalists who came in large numbers from East Bengal but immigrants from other parts of India, particularly the Bengali Hindus and the Marwari traders. Both groups occupied highly visible positions of apparent power and privilege in the civil service and in trade respectively. This bred resentment among native Assamese as, after Independence, they aspired to equal opportunities at a time when insufficient new jobs were being created to meet rapidly rising demands. Rather than fostering Assamese demands for separate statehood, this situation led instead to agitation for repatriation of non-Assamese and for economic opportunities to be restricted to local-born Assamese.

Such demands were not restricted to Assam, as the *mulki rules* ('sons of the soil') disputes in the Telengana region of Andhra Pradesh or the Jharkand movement in Bihar and Orissa demonstrated. If met, these claims would have carried deeply damaging implications for India's ability to contain its diversity within a united state. Internal migration within India has been widespread over generations, bringing the potential not only for competition but also for integration. All Indian citizens were given the constitutional right to 'adequate facilities' for primary education in their native tongue in whatever part of India they lived. Freedom to take up work anywhere in India was guaranteed, in part to encourage such integration. However, these rights and guarantees are also a direct recognition of the danger posed by the disruptive potential of sub-national identities.

The belief is widespread in Indian government circles that this diversity has been used by forces hostile to India to spread unrest in order to limit India's ability to sustain an independent domestic and foreign policy stance. The United States and China in particular have repeatedly been the object of bitter criticism for their supposed support of secessionist and opposition groups and movements, and the hand of the CIA has widely been seen in India as visible in trouble-spots from Tamil Nadu to Punjab. The latest in many examples of this phenomenon was the comment of K.N. Singh, General Secretary of the then governing Congress (I), who was quoted as claiming that 'American imperialism is behind the unrest in Kashmir, and Pakistan is unnecessarily getting involved in it.'[9] The potency of this fear should not be underestimated. The Indian writer and journalist K.N. Malik has suggested, for example, that problems in the Indian-British relationship in the 1980s stemmed in part from a belief in India that Britain was a safe haven and base for extraterritorial groups sending money and arms as well as giving political backing for Sikh militants. He argues that it is believed in some quarters that the British government was happy to see this as a means of bringing India to heel on some areas of international dispute between the two countries. Not surprisingly, such a view was totally rejected by the British government.

Foreign policy formation: the institutional structure

Nehru had argued that India's foreign policy flowed naturally and inevitably from the constellation of its national interests – social, political and economic. But it is rare for the 'national interest' to be perceived in a unitary way. By their nature multi-party democratic states experience divergent views on major policy issues. The ability of different groups to exert pressure in order to shape policies, including foreign policy, may have a vital bearing on the nature of international relations, just as it does on domestic concerns. However, India's experience suggests that while heated disputes have frequently characterized domestic political activity, foreign policy has been marked by a striking degree of political unity.

India is not unique in showing such a distinction between domestic and foreign policy. Lloyd Rudolph and Suzanne Rudolph, American authorities on Indian politics, have pointed to the differences in pressure group influence on policy between domestic and foreign affairs in the United States.[10] Yet Indian and US democratic institutions differ fundamentally. The parliamentary form of government and the bureaucratic framework India adopted from Britain at Independence ensure major contrasts in style and function. Both legally and politically,

> ... the Indian Union Parliament has authority and plays a role in the area of foreign policy very similar to that of the Parliament of the United Kingdom. Treaties and other international agreements may be negotiated and ratified by the executive without reference to Parliament. As in the UK, although they are legally binding on the state, they do not become part of domestic law unless legislation to that effect is passed by Parliament.'[11]

Again, as in the United Kingdom, the executive has complete

control over the appointment of diplomats and other foreign representatives. Thus the structures of foreign policy development are formally not dissimilar from their British model. The Foreign Ministry is headed by the Foreign Minister and two junior ministers. From the administrative service they are matched by a Foreign Secretary (the difference in nomenclature from the British system can be confusing) and Secretaries of State. From time to time there has been an influential Policy Planning Committee, though this is currently defunct, and parliament has what Nancy Jetly, an Indian political scientist, has called a 'somewhat nebulous role' in foreign policy-making. However, as she rightly points out,

> ... certain aspects of foreign policy, particularly those having a bearing on the country's internal problems and/or national security, are bound to generate considerable public interest, and Parliament as a mirror of popular feeling becomes an effective forum for the expression and exchange of a wide range of views which no government can fail to take cognizance of.[12]

But it is equally difficult to compare India's political structures and in particular the bearing they have on foreign policy-making directly with those of the United Kingdom. In India the prime minister and the prime minister's office have had an unequalled influence on foreign policy throughout the period since 1947, an influence which has remained intact through changes of government and which some would argue increased still further under Rajiv Gandhi. Towards the end of Rajiv Gandhi's period in office, Peter Lyon argued that:

> ... the top career professionals in External Affairs, Defence, and the Economic ministries probably are as competent as at any time in the past ... But there is reason to believe that some of them have become so demoralised or intimidated by the capriciousness of their political masters and the challenges of their times that it is unlikely that they can perform, or perhaps be invited to play, the central and constructive role their predecessors played in foreign policy formulation and execution in the past ... The Union Cabinet and the ruling 'party' are now so weak institutionally that they are incapable of formulating high policy properly. Rajiv Gandhi's personal secretariat (an institution which has wielded a strong and

decisive influence on policy making on many occasions in the past) may be presumed to carry considerable weight ... it is no empty hyperbole to speak of Rajiv's Raj.[13]

V.P. Singh has brought a marked change in style of government, but the weakness of his coalition administration has made it impossible to see clearly the form of the new decision-making process.

Formally, the cabinet has a dominant position in policy-making, although, despite the lack of standing parliamentary committees on foreign affairs, parliament does consider foreign policy questions. During Nehru's period in office there was no effective institutional base for analysing and shaping policy, but there were various external forces which had a bearing on the foreign policy pursued. After 1962 not the least of these was the democratic process itself, for while neither parliament nor the very nebulous 'public opinion' exposed foreign policy to any kind of strategic influence, large-scale failures could have severe political repercussions.

As Mrs Gandhi found later in the wake of the 1971 war with Pakistan, success could also bring rich political harvests. However, the policy became even further removed from the cabinet. Under Prime Minister Shastri, 'the Prime Minister's Secretariat emerged as an alternative source to the Cabinet of advice, influence and power in the executive branch of government'.[14] The prime minister's secretariat underwent fluctuating fortunes under Mrs Gandhi, and personal advisers played a vital part in her government's decision-making as they did under Rajiv Gandhi until his defeat in November 1989.

Alongside these advisers, a range of extra-parliamentary institutions came to play an increasing part in influencing foreign policy decisions, from the Research and Analysis Wing (RAW), India's secret service, through to the armed services. Perhaps the most striking feature of the role of India's armed services is the extent to which they have been kept outside the policy-making process. P.R. Brass has shown that 'In India an early alliance developed between the politicians and the civilian bureaucracy to control the military.' All three military chiefs remain subordinate to the civilian Defence Minister, and the 'potential for military intervention in Indian politics remains low. There has never been an attempted military coup in India. Even if the will were present, the obstacles to effective intervention are formidable.'[15]

The workings of India's foreign policy bureaucracy, however, have been described by Richard Cronin, a highly experienced American observer, as 'byzantine', and the precise role of close political advisers to the prime minister as 'nebulous'.[16] Nevertheless, now as in the days of Rajiv Gandhi's grandfather, the prime minister and his advisers hold the key to developing and implementing foreign policy. *India Today* argued in May 1988 that the cabinet secretariat 'during the last three years has emerged as the most powerful arm of government ... through which the Prime Minister wields his power and is able to bypass, even overrule his ministerial colleagues without prior consultation.'[17] In fact the overriding power of India's prime minister in foreign policy-making and implementation goes back all the way to Independence.

One of the more interesting questions following Rajiv Gandhi's electoral defeat in November 1989 was whether both the institutions of foreign policy-making and foreign policy itself would undergo fundamental change. Expectations of radical change accompanied the election of the Janata Party in 1977, but were rapidly muted. Although foreign policy played a marginal role in the November 1989 election campaign, the National Front made a point of emphasizing its determination to improve relations with India's neighbours and to strengthen non-alignment. V.P. Singh himself has constantly stressed his firm intention to move away from the personalized form of government which he attacked as Rajiv's style. The first year of the new government has shown clearly that there has been a major change in the style of leadership. Furthermore, the radical restructuring of power in the Soviet Union and Eastern Europe is forcing new questions˙ onto the Indian government's foreign policy agenda. But, as its response to the crisis in Kashmir suggests, there is no evidence yet that it has been able to break away from the regional imperatives which have so often shaped India's foreign policies.

Conclusion

Domestic pressures have borne heavily on India's foreign policy with respect both to its immediate neighbours and to wider relationships. Non-alignment, the most basic premise of India's global foreign-policy stance, could also be argued to stem directly from the nature of India's cultural traditions. Nehru himself argued that 'non-alignment is a policy inherent in the whole mental outlook of India, inherent in the conditioning of the Indian mind'.

Writing for the International Institute of Strategic Studies, S. Chubin termed such a view the 'theology of non-alignment'. He went on to argue that in practice non-alignment was more concerned with protecting India's 'self-perceived role as the legitimately dominant regional power' than with the pursuit of high-minded ideals. As a means of keeping the military presence of the superpowers out of the Indian Ocean and the South Asian region, Chubin saw non-alignment as serving the purpose of enhancing India's own freedom of political and military action.

Certainly, between 1971 and 1977, and then again from 1979 until her assassination, Mrs Gandhi acted from time to time as if India's role could be that of 'regional policeman'. Rajiv Gandhi's decision to send the Indian Navy to the Maldives in 1988 was in direct line of descent from such thinking. One of India's major objectives since 1971 has been to keep superpower conflict out of its region. To that extent non-alignment has served immediate political objectives. But in no sense was non-alignment an ideological underpinning for a *realpolitik* of establishing regional dominance. India's own perception of its regional policy is self-protective and defensive. It is one of the paradoxes of the region that the view of India as the dominant regional power is universally shared by its neighbours but totally disavowed by India itself.

In Indian eyes non-alignment has given the country a prestige and influence in the wider world the impact of which in domestic terms may be difficult to assess but which is undoubtedly regarded as important within India. The continuing commitment to non-alignment through changes of government is striking testimony to that fact.

4

ECONOMIC INTERESTS AND FOREIGN POLICY

The hallmark of India's economy today is its growing diversity and complexity. The often repeated claims that India is the world's tenth largest industrial economy probably imply too much. [1] As the World Development Report for 1988 makes clear, for example, in terms of the total value added in manufacturing India ranked thirteenth in 1985 compared with fifteenth in 1971. In terms of per capita output, of course, the position is very much lower.

Many within India and outside are critical of the rates of economic growth actually achieved, but the economic challenges facing the government of independent India were daunting. George Blyn suggested that in 1947 India had experienced fifty years of agricultural stagnation, and the steady and increasing rate of population growth meant that millions were barely touched by new industrial opportunities. While the cities of Bombay and Calcutta, Ahmadabad and Madras had all experienced some industrial growth, the total industrial employment in India in 1947 was 1.7 million – less than that of Greater London. This was out of a total population of 360 million, compared with the United Kingdom's population of 55 million. [2]

In three fields the domestic problems of achieving rapid economic growth have been interleaved with foreign policy interests: aid, trade, and the attraction of inward investment for industrial expansion. Indian foreign policy has been shaped significantly by the need to maximize economic growth while sacrificing as little political and economic independence as possible.

In seeking to achieve these twin objectives India has developed extensive contacts outside its Asian region. In the last decade India's economic policy has undergone a major change in emphasis, opening the doors to inward investment and joint ventures. Pursuit of economic goals has led it greatly to extend its contacts with the European Community, now by far its most important trading partner, with the Soviet Union and with the United States. Diversification – of sources of aid, of trading partners and the composition of trade, and of partners for industrial collaboration – has been the thread running through India's widening economic relationships as it has attempted to achieve both its economic and political goals of development.

The economic challenge

While the seeds of economic modernization had been sown by 1971, the challenge of mass poverty remained untackled. The British economist Professor Michael Lipton argued in 1968 that 'even an almost incredible growth performance in India – 5.5% p.a. till 1985 – will leave one in ten Indians destitute'.[3] As Appadorai has remarked, therefore, it is not surprising that 'the economic development of India has been such an urgent need that policy makers [used] foreign policy as a tool to further that development'.[4]

Such economic development was seen by the Indian government as desirable not just as a means of tackling poverty and increasing the general well-being of the population, but also as a strategy for strengthening India's independence of action in its own region and in the wider world. Thus while economic concerns have in no sense dominated foreign policy-making, in key areas of foreign relations they have had a significant bearing on India's priorities.

Energy needs

Development created enormous demands not only for capital, but also for technology. Energy needs have spiralled, commercial energy consumption rising more than eightfold in the thirty years after the beginning of the Second Five-Year Plan in 1956. Between 1971 and 1988 electricity generation increased from 61 billion KwH to 217 billion KwH. Agriculture's share of the use of electricity during the same period (largely for pumping irrigation water) doubled to 20.7%. Yet despite the threefold increase in production nearly every state was suffering significant power shortages in 1987–8. The overall deficit in that year was 10.9%,[5] and in some states it was as great as 30%.

Energy requirements for development face India with a cruel dilemma. In 1974–5 (the latest year for which figures are published) 195 million tonnes of coal substitute came from non-commercial sources – firewood, agricultural waste and cow dung.[6] This was nearly 44% of India's total energy requirement, and each of these fuels represented a costly loss of environmental resources which could have been used in better ways than burning. The ecological costs of forest clearance may not be fully understood but are widely believed to be severe, and the burning of cow dung (which alone accounts for nearly 7% of all energy consumed) represents a further loss.

As development progresses and population increases, even greater stress is being placed on domestic energy sources of coal, oil and hydroelectricity. Since 1985 the Soviet Union has offered large-scale credits for various energy programmes – a 2,400 MW hydroelectric station in Tehri, and assistance for digging new coal mines and oil exploration. Further advances of credit for conventional power developments were made in 1987 and agreement has been reached to build a 1,000 MW nuclear power station.[7] The gap between projected demand and internally available resources for energy is giving extra impetus to India's nuclear power programme. Conventional sources of energy have absorbed huge investments, as has the development of nuclear power.

India's push to create a significant nuclear power capacity, which initially enjoyed international support from Canada, the United States and Britain, became the focus of international concern after the explosion of a nuclear device in Rajasthan in 1974. Canada cut off all technological assistance, and during the late 1970s the United States under President Carter tried to put pressure on successive Indian governments to guarantee that they would not make nuclear weapons and to sign the Non-Proliferation Treaty. Although the interruption of supplies slowed India's programme, it has gone ahead, using entirely indigenous technology to bring on stream the nuclear plant at Kalpakkam, near Madras, in 1983. However, the programme is still beset by fundamental operating problems,[8] and although it continues to enjoy full political support, there are serious doubts as to the speed with which its contribution to meeting electricity needs in India will be sustained.

The green revolution and its effects

While the need for energy has grown, the demand for rapid agricultural change has also been profound. India entered the 1970s with the catastrophic harvest failures of the mid-1960s leading some observers to suggest that it would be the first major country to witness a Malthusian-style famine within the decade. By 1961 the total cropped area was 153 million hectares (50% of the total area). The expansion of land under cultivation, which had accounted for most of the increased agricultural output in the 1950s, was coming to a halt. Thus between 1951 and 1975 the agricultural area expanded at a rate of 1.2% per annum, but between 1976 and 1988 the rate of increase was down to 0.09% per annum. By 1988 the total cropped area was 57% of the total area.[9] Pressure on the land has continued throughout the 1970s and 1980s, and the urgency of increasing agricultural output by raising yields from land already under cultivation has grown remorselessly.

The challenge has been faced in part by a radical transformation of agricultural technology. But green revolution technology, which has underpinned the increase of India's agricultural production, has been heavily dependent on petrochemicals for fertilizer and pesticide. As a result India has struggled to find new and growing export markets to pay for rapidly increasing imports and to finance its own investment.

Investment policies

Despite some changes in industrial strategy during the 1970s, the major controls of government planning remained intact even through the period of Janata Party rule between 1977 and 1979, when some had expected a greater openness to the free market under the prime ministership of Morarji Desai. Indeed, the election of the Janata government was followed by the appointment of the socialist George Fernandes as Minister for Industry, and a tightening of controls on foreign investment in India. Large American companies like Coca-Cola were forced out of India altogether, highly publicized attempts being made to produce indigenous alternatives.

After Mrs Gandhi's return to power in 1979 India began subtly to change tack and tried increasingly hard to attract inward investment. Mrs Gandhi made it clear that she saw the need to liberalize aspects of India's industrial economy – a change of direction which received a substantial boost from Rajiv Gandhi when he took office in 1984. While there has been a significant streamlining of India's industrial licensing requirements since the 1984 election, alongside other developments in the field of economic planning, the implications for India's patterns of both inward and outward investment remain in the area of possibilities rather than of substantial achievement.

However, following V.P. Singh's first budget in 1985 (when he was Finance Minister), and under Rajiv Gandhi's constant urging, India's economic strategy started to shift from the highly centralized socialist planning of the first three Five-Year Plans to a less rigidly structured, more liberal and less tightly controlled framework. Although foreign capital continued to play a part in the private sector of India's economy after Independence, since 1971 a renewed interest was shown by the government in attracting funds not only from non-resident Indians living abroad but also from companies to share in joint ventures.

Nevertheless it could be argued that right up to the present India's economic development strategy has been subordinated to the political goal of avoiding national dependence upon either foreign powers or multinational corporations. And even when the national government has taken steps to ease restrictions on foreign investment in India, middle-level officials and state governments have dragged their feet.

Foreign aid

The search for economic as well as political independence led the first governments of India to adopt economic goals that would maximize India's control over its economy, within what was seen as a socialist framework of ownership and planning. The Second Five-Year Plan set down a strategic framework which identified a wide range of industrial sectors, notably in capital goods industries, in which the public sector would have sole operation, alongside further sectors in which private-sector investment would be allowed either alongside the public sector or on its own.

The apparatus of central planning, with strict rules governing trade and industrial licensing policy, has dominated India's economy since the early 1950s. But in addition to establishing a means of central government control, the Plans also envisaged a massive overall increase in investment. Successive Indian governments have looked to foreign aid as a vital means of contributing to that investment, although the role of aid in development has been controversial both for economic theorists and for development planners and politicians in India. The complexities of definition, and the extent to which aid is interrelated with non-economic assistance, add to the difficulties of analysing its contribution to development. Thus as Peter Duncan, a British specialist on Soviet-Indian relations, has shown for example, while Soviet aid to India up to 1985 comprised less than 5% of India's total, compared to the 50% of the OECD countries, its concentration on capital projects has made it responsible, according to Soviet estimates, for the production of one-third of India's steel and aluminium, nearly half of its power and mining equipment and nearly 80% of its metallurgical equipment.[10] However, as Duncan goes on to note, it is often impossible to separate aid from trade, as much Soviet-Indian trade has in effect been in the form of bartering, prices being fixed in rupees rather than hard currency. Since the 1958 trade agreement between India and the Soviet Union no foreign exchange has been used, and Soviet loans were made repayable through the export of goods. In contrast, much American aid, including the PL480 programme, which gave aid in the form of convertible currency units, concentrated on meeting urgent food needs and consumption goods. Between these two extremes fall a wide range of both project and non-project aid schemes.[11]

When public ownership was intended to provide both the means of effective planning for economic growth and the guarantee of political independence from external economic control (such as it was feared would be exercised by a private sector dominated by foreign-owned capital), it may seem ironic that India had to look overseas for a major component of its investment capital. In the Second and Third Five-Year Plans this came largely from foreign aid.

Lipton and Toye have argued that while the facts about aid and India's economic performance since Independence are clear, 'they are also counter-intuitive. Most intelligent laymen probably believe: 1. That aid to India has been large; 2. that India's growth performance has been bad; 3. that this is partially due to substantial, and rather successful, policy emphasis on equity and poverty alleviation at the cost of growth; and 4. that aid played a major role in both the growth outcome and the equity outcome'.

They argue that the first three propositions are almost completely false. In 1986 India was indeed the largest recipient of aid in the world.[12] But while it received 7% of global net aid disbursements to developing countries, it had nearly 21% of their total population. In per capita terms it received only $2.60 in 1986.[13] Further, by 1986 aid was far less important to India than it had been twenty years earlier. Allowing for inflation, the peak of aid receipts was in the Third Plan period, 1961–6. Although there were subsequent peaks in 1974 and again in 1980, aid disbursements in 1984–5 were half the levels of those in 1974–6 for a population that was 20% greater. Table 4.1 shows aid received since Independence, in real terms.

Table 4.1   External assistance utilized since Independence (Rs crore)

Period	Loans	Grants	Total
To end 4th Plan	8573	713	9285
1974–78	5919	1157	7077
1979–83	8207	1693	9900
1984–88	12209	1710	13919

Source: Government of India, *Economic Survey 1988–89*.
Note: 1 crore = 10 million.

As the figures quoted above suggest, there has been a major decline in the relative importance of aid to the Indian economy. In the mid-1980s the contribution of aid to total savings was less than 3%, half that of the early 1970s (see Figure 4.1), and the contribution of aid to government investment fell from over 50% in the late 1960s to 10% in the mid-1980s. At the same time the contribution of non-aid foreign savings grew steadily, by the mid-1980s reaching 7% of total savings, nearly double the figure for aid.[14]

The economic rationale for seeking large-scale aid flows in the 1950s and 1960s seemed self-evident from the poverty of domestic resources. However, critics such as P.T. Bauer argue that the inflow of resources in the form of aid has been misallocated and encouraged waste and slow growth. Lipton and Toye, in contrast, show

Figure 4.1 Aid as % domestic savings

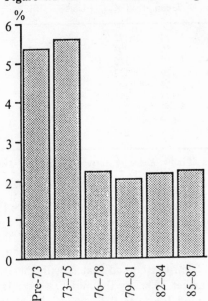

that, in the early period of planning, aid 'played an important role in permitting public and corporate investment to take place well ahead of the development of the household sector's propensity to save'.[15]

The argument over the effectiveness of aid need not detain us. But alongside its economic importance, aid has had telling political implications. Mrs Gandhi recognized the potential negative political conditions of aid when she said: 'No country should even think of using aid to make India change its fundamental policies. If any country has such ideas, it is nurturing wrong notions.'[16] In practice it has proved impossible to have 'string-free' assistance, whether from individual countries or from multilateral agencies such as the World Bank and the IMF. Furthermore, the aid offered has not always been appropriate, and as in the case, for example, of the British-provided Westland helicopters, has appeared in some eyes to benefit the donor at least as much as the receiver.[17]

Partly in order to reduce dependency on a single bloc or individual donor, India has sought to diversify its sources of aid and to look increasingly towards the multilateral donors of the World Bank and

Table 4.2 Utilization of aid to India since 1971, by source (Rs crore)

Date	FRG	Japan	UK	USA	USSR	IBRD	IDA
1980–1	144	90	197	82	33	139	522
1981–2	127	36	203	70	23	377	693
1982–3	137	128	160	30	40	287	1085
1983–4	115	139	122	76	75	486	900
1984–5	127	68	188	53	108	344	980
1985–6	147	175	195	70	161	395	1198
1986–7	260	409	200	127	176	801	1011
1987–8	257	628	131	123	222	1659	1207
1988–9	424	588	235	99	307	1409	1273

Source: Government of India, *Economic Survey of India, 1988–89.*

particularly the soft loan facilities of the IDA. Since 1971 there have been major changes in the sources of India's aid funds, shown in Table 4.2 and Figure 4.2.

Up to the Fourth Plan (1969–74) over 40% of India's external assistance came from the United States, with the IBRD and IDA contributing a further 19%. By the mid-1980s the IBRD and IDA assistance accounted for over 50%, while the United States was contributing directly well under 10% of the total.[18] Duncan has observed that although India was the largest beneficiary of Soviet aid in the developing world, not only was the total aid given comparatively small but in every year between 1967 and 1981, with the exception of 1973, interest repayments to the Soviet Union were greater than the volume of aid disbursed.[19] The dramatic surge in Soviet aid since 1986 reflects the new Soviet assistance for major energy projects discussed above.

Diversification of sources has been the key to India's aid policy. Even so, India has sometimes found itself constrained either in the use of aid offered to it or in overall economic management. In 1966 it experienced that pressure in its strongest form when the IMF and the United States insisted on a devaluation of the rupee by over 36%.

Trade
Some of the rhetoric associated with the Second and Third Five-Year Plans suggested that India was attempting to achieve economic autarky. Despite the strict controls on domestic industrial activity

Figure 4.2 Aid from USA, USSR, IBRD and IDA (Rs crore)

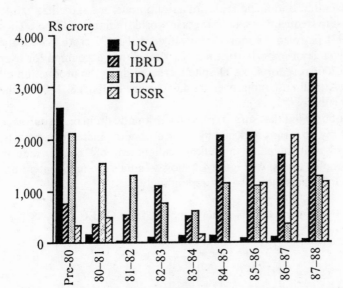

and on the patterns of international trade allowed under planning regulations, complete autonomy was never an objective of Indian economic planning. The element of pragmatism grew stronger in the 1980s, however, as the government sought to liberalize its internal economy and its links with the international markets.

It would of course be misleading to suggest either that domestic economic policy or changing patterns of trade themselves have dictated India's foreign policy since 1971. However, India has made a systematic attempt to diversify its patterns of trade, both in terms of commodities traded and of trading partners. The Confederation of Engineering Industry comments that

> ... we now have trading links with virtually all the countries and the commodities traded. India's exports currently comprise a wide range of agricultural and industrial items, project exports which include consultancy, civil construction, and turnkey projects ... the bulk of imports now consist of sophisticated machines, scarce raw materials, lubricants, oils and fertilisers which are required for the country's industrial and agricultural development.[20]

The dramatic surge in the cost of oil imports since 1971 illustrates the fact that trading policy is not autonomous, and India has had to adjust to frequently rapid changes in world trading conditions. Thus in 1971 petroleum imports were valued at Rs 137 crore, 8% of the total value of imports. Just ten years later they accounted for over Rs 5,200 crore, or 42%. Despite increased domestic production oil imports still cost India over Rs 4,050 crore in 1987–8, 18% of the import bill.[21]

Not only did that surge represent a dramatic drain on resources in itself, by no means matched by a corresponding increase in exports; it also contributed to a radical realignment of India's trade in geographic terms. As Figure 4.3 shows, India's economic interest in the Gulf states increased correspondingly.

Figure 4.3   % India's imports from OPEC 1960–88

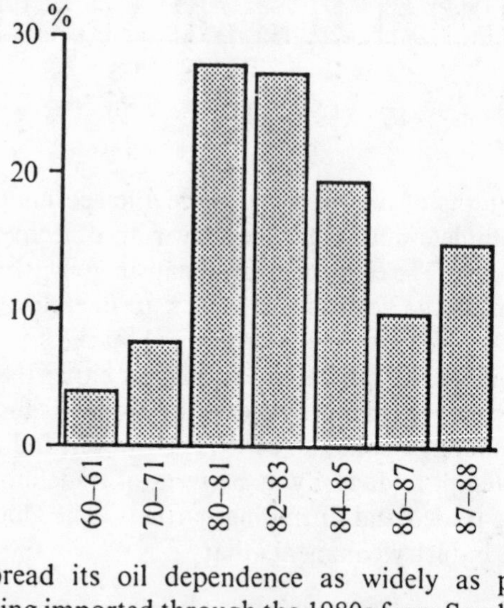

India spread its oil dependence as widely as possible, large volumes being imported through the 1980s from Saudi Arabia, Iran, Iraq and Kuwait, in addition to comparatively cheap supplies from the Soviet Union. As was shown in Chapter 3, such economic links reinforced other foreign policy objectives, and the need to remain on good terms with as wide a range of Middle Eastern Islamic states as possible has been strengthened by the rapidly rising internal demands for energy. The peak of this demand has now been passed, and India's own oil production provided over 30 million tonnes of

Figure 4.4 Exports: major categories 1960–88 (Rs crore)

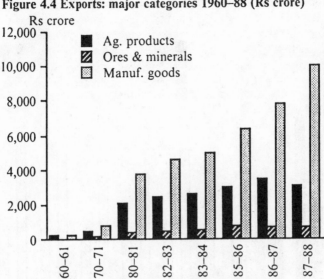

the 45 million tonnes consumed in 1987–8; but the rapid increase in energy demand will make continued large-scale imports necessary. Thus while oil imports from Iraq and Iran dropped from their peak values of Rs 884 crore and Rs 1,339 crore respectively in 1980–1 to Rs 373 crore and Rs 120 crore in 1987–8, imports from Saudi Arabia had picked up again in 1987–8 to a near-record high of Rs 1,387 crore.[22]

Oil imports dominated the quantitative pattern of change in trade in the 1970s and 1980s, but there have been other significant developments. Liberalization of the economy and the speeding-up of industrial development has meant that the import of machinery and raw materials unobtainable in India has risen sharply. Machinery and transport equipment accounted for over Rs 5,000 crore in 1986–7, and a further Rs 1,500 crore for iron and steel.[23]

The importance of India's exports to its wider economic achievements has been a constant source of concern to the government. As Figure 4.4 shows, the value of exported manufactured goods has climbed steadily since 1970–1. By far the largest single element in this trade has been cotton textiles. It is not surprising that India

Figure 4.5 Major exports as % of total exports 1960–87

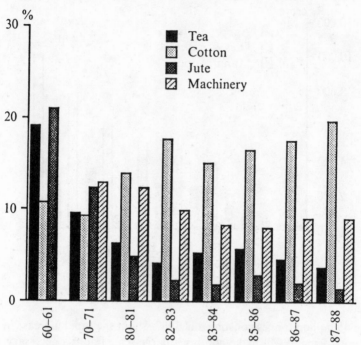

should have played a leading role in international trade negotiations, as in the successive UN Conferences on Trade and Development and the Multi-Fibre Agreements. It has consistently tried to coordinate support for its positions on Third World trade within both the United Nations and the Non-Aligned Movement. That it has few significant major successes to its credit is a reflection less of the failure of its diplomacy than of the strength of the negotiating position of the OECD countries.

Despite the increase in manufactured exports and the changing composition of India's export trade, progress towards exporting significant quantities of engineering and other comparatively high-technology manufactured goods has been very slow. As Figure 4.5 shows, in 1987–8 the export of machinery accounted for less than 10% of total exports, and although tea and jute exports together had declined from 40% of exports in 1960–1 to less than 5% in 1987–8,

Figure 4.6 % Imports from major trading blocs

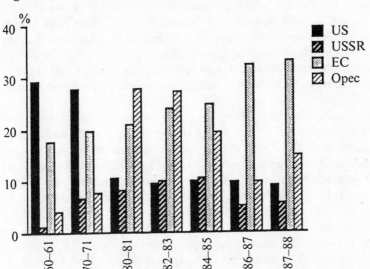

their place had largely been taken by cotton manufactures. Efforts to diversify rapidly during the 1980s were constantly thwarted not just by international trade barriers but by the relatively poor quality and high cost of many Indian manufactured goods, protected in the domestic market from international competition by high tariffs and wide-ranging import restrictions.

Diversification of India's trading partners has been just as important a part of successive governments' strategies as has diversification of sources of aid, and for similar reasons. While in absolute terms trade with all India's traditional trading partners has increased, their relative share has undergone contrasting fortunes. This is particularly evident when India's patterns of trade with the world's four major trading blocs – the United States, the European Community, OPEC and the USSR – are examined.

The most striking changes between groups have been the rise of the European Community both in absolute and relative terms as a source of India's imports and a decline in the relative importance of the United States (see Figure 4.6). In 1960, for example, imports from the United States accounted for nearly 30% of the total, and those from the European Community a further 19%. Of this figure, however, the United Kingdom alone contributed 16%. By 1970 the United States still accounted for nearly 28%, though the United Kingdom's share had already dropped to under 8%. Since then the US share has dropped to around 10% while the United Kingdom's varied between 5% and 8% in the 1980s. By contrast, the share of the European Community in India's imports in 1988 rose to over 33%.

No single trading partner has taken the place of either the United Kingdom or the United States. However, successive trade agreements with the Soviet Union enabled it to expand exports more rapidly than many Western countries. Thus in absolute terms imports to India from the USSR rose over 16 times between 1970–1 and 1985–6, whereas those from Britain rose tenfold and from the United States less than fivefold. But perhaps the most striking individual comparison can be made with Japan, which achieved an increase of more than twenty times in the same period.

Other OECD countries also expanded exports to India comparatively fast, and in 1985–6 the OECD countries as a whole accounted for five times the value of the imports originating from Eastern Europe, a similar ratio to that fifteen years previously. In contrast, the total value of the OPEC countries' share rose thirty times in the fifteen-year period.

The most important apparent contrast between the major trading blocs, in terms of the volume of their trade with India, is Eastern Europe's seeming trade deficit in India's favour throughout the period since 1971. This reflects the fact that the official statistics exclude arms flows from the Soviet Union to India. Despite the often easy terms and cheap credit made available by the Soviet Union for such purchases, they have represented a very substantial concealed import for India.[24]

Exports have been particularly important in India's attempts to earn capital and keep its balance of payments under control. Despite an expansion in the 1970s in African and Middle Eastern markets, notably for engineering goods, India experienced considerable difficulties in these markets throughout the 1980s. In part this reflects the problems caused by the Gulf war, especially in India's exports of machinery and equipment to Iran, but the problem also lies in the uncompetitiveness and uneven quality control, by international standards, of much of India's output. In contrast, exports of gems and of garments have been booming, leading all other export commodities.

As for India's intra-regional trade, by far the most striking feature is its almost total insignificance. Apart from India's vital role as a route for the trade of Nepal and Bhutan, it has hardly any trade with its neighbours. Only partly does this reflect a lack of complementarity between India and the other members of the South Asian Association for Regional Cooperation (SAARC). Before Partition in 1947 regions that are now in Pakistan and Bangladesh had strong trade links with regions that are now in India. The climate of political distrust that surrounded Partition, the fear in Pakistan of the power of Indian industry to prevent any industrial take-off as a result of its comparatively advanced state, and the almost complete break in trade from 1949 have resulted in minimal economic ties between the countries of the subcontinent.

Political sensitivity to India's economic power remains a potent political factor in its trade with all its neighbours. Within weeks of the creation of Bangladesh in 1971, Indian traders were the butt of fierce Bangladeshi hostility. The political upheavals which shook Sri Lanka as it neared the second anniversary of the Indo-Sri Lankan Accord on 29 July 1989 were marked by threats to any shopkeeper selling Indian goods. And as the *Far Eastern Economic Review* reported in 1987, under General Zia Pakistan 'unilaterally confined imports from India to public sector agencies and put restrictions on its private sector in this regard'. Out of Pakistan's total import bill in 1985–6 of Rs 66.7 million, just Rs 100,000 were spent on goods from India, and the value of Pakistani exports to India amounted to a bare Rs 500,000.[25] In the cautiously warming relationship between Pakistan and India there is scope for significant advance in mutual trade, but there is no sign yet of any major development.

Investment

By contrast there have been indications of a new international interest in the long-term potential of the Indian economy as a future market and as one of the world's most important economic regions in which to invest, as India's GNP grew at over 4% per annum between 1976 and 1988.[26]

International responses to that opportunity have varied greatly, from the Japanese involvement in car manufacturing and relatively high-technology electronics to the continuing Soviet interest in large-scale heavy industry. At the same time India's attempts to develop a wide-ranging defence industry have led to large-scale collaboration with other powers, notably the Soviet Union, but also a widening range of Western countries including the United States.

The recent expansion and liberalization of the Indian economy has been watched with interest in the United States. Indeed, the coolness of the official relationship between that country and India has been partially offset by the willingness of US companies, particularly in the field of high technology, to invest in India: the comparatively high-tech nature of US-Indian trade is well recognized.

The attention that was focused on the success of the then Foreign Secretary, A.P. Venkateshwaran, in negotiating an improved deal on the Cray supercomputer in early 1987 illustrated the potential for developing such links, though problems remain on both sides. In part the potential stems from the presence of up to 600,000 highly qualified Indians living in the United States. Many in this largely professional group retain their close links with India. The economic ties that have followed these personal links have tended to favour the 'industries of the future'. None the less, American exposure to India is still comparatively slight. Sen Gupta pointed out that in 1985 total US investment in India was in the order of $500,000. This compares with $2 billion in Hong Kong, $1.3 billion in Indonesia and $1.24 billion in the Philippines.[27] In contrast, India's non-oil trading links with the Soviet Union have been dominated by iron- and steel-based industries. Thus in 1985–6 India exported engineering goods worth a total of Rs 10 billion, 20% of which went to the Soviet Union, compared with 10% to the United States and 3% to Britain.

Although there has been no dramatic boom in inward investment to India, as some had forecast following Rajiv Gandhi's highly successful visit to the United States in 1985, investment has grown significantly. Since 1984 the United States has been consistently the largest investor, putting in Rs 0.89 crore in 1984, Rs 3.99 crore in 1985 and Rs 2.99 crore in each of 1986 and 1987, a total of over Rs 10 crore. It is striking that non-resident Indians were the most important single external source of investment funds, providing more than any individual country apart from the United States, at over Rs 6 crore. They were followed by the Federal Republic of

Germany (Rs 4.47 crore), Japan (Rs 3.44 crore) and the United Kingdom (Rs 2.2 crore).[28] India certainly sees joint ventures as one of the most promising avenues of international economic cooperation. In July 1989 the Director of the Confederation of Engineering Industry said that over 2,000 new joint ventures had been approved, mainly with members of the European Community, in the first six months of the year.

Nevertheless foreign investment in India has continued to lag far behind that in other developing Asian economies. In 1988, for example, it amounted to only just over one-tenth of foreign investment in Taiwan. The government of V.P. Singh appears to be proceeding very cautiously with the liberalization of regulations governing inward investment, particularly the rule that in general foreigners should not own more than 40 per cent of local companies.[29]

Defence equipment deals

Just as the explosion of a nuclear device at Pokharan in 1974 dramatized India's potential military power in the region, so the launching of Agni, its first intermediate-range rocket, in June 1989 symbolized the rapid progress it is making towards securing indigenous defence capabilities. And yet since 1971 India has remained dependent on a wide range of imported arms for all its services, from the purchase of the two second-hand aircraft carriers from the United Kingdom, the Vikrant and the Viraat, in the 1980s, through Jaguars, Sea Harriers and MiGs – the most recent of which, the MiG-29 and MiG-31, are going into production in India even before being offered to the Soviet Union's Warsaw Pact allies.[30]

Despite the difficulties in obtaining accurate and reliable information about India's arms purchases, it is clear that the Soviet Union's rise to the position of supplier of up to 65% of India's defence equipment in the late 1980s has overshadowed other developments, with transfers worth up to $4,200 million, according to CIA estimates.[31] Duncan suggests that price discounts of as much as 50% have more than compensated for lack of sophistication compared with equivalent armoury from the West, an attraction which is further enhanced by repayment in goods rather than in hard currency. He has documented the scale of India's current dependence on Soviet weaponry, and the strategic importance of

57

such a defence link is obvious. However, while successive Indian governments since 1971 have sustained attempts to diversify the country's arms procurement programme – evidenced in the purchase of Mirages from France and the Anglo-French Jaguars – it is equally clear that India's decision to opt for Soviet weaponry as the major source of supply has been propelled at least as much by economic advantage as by coincidence of strategic interests.

Conclusion

Despite the rapid growth of India's economy, particularly in the last half of the 1980s, and the enormous economic potential of an integrated economy with over 800 million people, India still remains far from being a world power in the global economic system. Although it plays a prominent part in the world's multilateral economic forums, such as UNCTAD and GATT, its contribution to world trade, both of goods and invisibles, is still far too small to be influential. Yet if the transformation of its economic policies and performance continues into the 1990s, it has the potential to play a far fuller role in the world economic system.

Today one of the most striking features of India's economic role in its South Asian region is the almost total lack of economic links with its neighbours. The development of common economic objectives has to wait on the resolution of the political issues which remain the key to understanding relations within South Asia and to India's foreign policy with respect to its neighbours. These are the subject of Chapter 5.

5

INDIA AS A REGIONAL POWER

India lies at the heart of its subcontinental region, which in the British period had been part of what Leo Rose has called 'an integrated foreign policy system'. Rose argues that the primary purpose of India's regional policy has been 'to extract, in some form or another, recognition of India's hegemonistic status in the region from both of the major external powers, and from its neighbours in the region.'[1] However, although India has undoubtedly sought a pre-eminent leadership position in South Asia, its ultimate objective has been self-protection rather than aggressive or territorial expansionism.

India's foreign policy with respect to its immediate neighbours has pursued almost entirely political rather than economic interests. In theory, India has since 1971 retained its commitment to non-violent resolution of conflict and non-interference in the internal affairs of other South Asian states. Yet as was shown in Chapter 3, when India's vital interests were seen to be at stake such detachment was always going to be difficult. In the 1980s India became deeply affected by the Islamization of Pakistani politics, the tide of fundamentalism in Afghanistan and the upsurge of Tamil nationalism in Sri Lanka, to mention just three examples of developments in neighbouring South Asian states which have a direct bearing on India's internal security interests. In this chapter India's relations with Pakistan and Sri Lanka are discussed in order to illustrate these regional pressures.

Great inequalities of size and economic strength pose inevitable problems for relationships between neighbouring states. Compared to Europe, where nation states such as Denmark or Switzerland, with populations of under five million, have successfully maintained a large measure of national independence, the fear that national integrity in South Asia could be compromised by India's size might seem overstated. Pakistan and Bangladesh each claim more than 100 million citizens, while even Nepal and Sri Lanka both have populations of more than fifteen million.

Yet even Bangladesh feels almost incomparably weak in relation to India. When there are conflicts of interest, as over the sharing of water from the Ganges, or migration into Assam, Bangladesh sees itself surrounded by India's land mass to the east, north and west, with Indian naval power now uncontestable in the Bay of Bengal to the south. Similarly Nepal, consistently trying to walk the tightrope between Indian and Chinese power, has faced a constant struggle to maintain national independence. The 1989 dispute was only the latest in repeated periods of tension.

To many outside observers India is clearly the dominant regional power in South Asia. India, however, sees itself as part of a wider region which includes China. Indeed, since 1962 China has been of far greater long-term strategic significance to India than either the almost complete absence of economic links between the two countries or the weakness of their diplomatic ties would suggest. China, the third point of the triangle between India's essentially South Asian regional concerns and its relations with the superpowers, has played a strategic role in India's foreign policy thinking. The difficulties of border delimitation through the Himalayas give concrete shape to the complex problems that remain to be resolved between the neighbouring giants. Sino-Indian relations will be treated in more detail in the third section of this chapter.

India and Pakistan

Over coffee at an international military seminar on South Asian current affairs, held in London in 1987, a high-ranking US army officer asked: 'Why is India so paranoid about Pakistan? India is a giant in the region, Pakistan comparatively tiny. What on earth does India have to fear?' While paranoia is a far-fetched description of the Indian attitude, it is a fact that Pakistan remains at the centre of India's foreign policy concerns in the region.

For a short period after India's 1971 military victory it seemed that relations might improve. Mrs Gandhi, riding the crest of a powerful wave of domestic political support, was inclined to be magnanimous. Recognizing the major change in geopolitical balance that the creation of Bangladesh had brought about, she started on the slow process of reconciliation. The situation in Pakistan was also favourable, for although Zulfikar Ali Bhutto had been one of India's fiercest critics in Pakistan during the 1960s, the trauma of defeat for the Pakistani military government had brought him to power in a totally new political context, when the future viability of even the truncated Pakistan was at stake. Lawrence Ziring suggests that Bhutto's intense hostility to India during this period was 'predicated on maximizing the fear of India in order to keep his detractors from further fractioning the state'.[2] The immediate domestic political realities in Pakistan in 1972 were certainly radically different from those of the late 1960s, allowing the promise of normalization to be seen as in Pakistan's basic interest.

The Simla Accord (signed on 3 July 1972 by Prime Minister Indira Gandhi and President Bhutto), with its promise of normalizing relations and developing a constructive relationship, marked a commitment to resolve all conflicts by peaceful means. In signing the Accord President Bhutto also accepted that contentious issues, including that of Kashmir, would be resolved without resort to international or third-party mediation. Nevertheless progress in building that relationship was slow. In part that reflected the unease with which Pakistan viewed the greatly strengthened friendship between India and the Soviet Union which was marked by the Indo-Soviet Treaty. Pakistan's attempts to strengthen ties with the People's Republic of China were an effort to counter that strategic link with a balancing axis.

The lack of practical Chinese help for Pakistan in the 1971 war had left many in Pakistan with doubts about the reliability of China as an ally in the face of a threat from India. To Indians the refusal of the Chinese to be drawn into that war suggested that they had successfully been faced down – some compensation for the 1962 humiliation. But Pakistan's doubts did not deter either Bhutto's government or the subsequent government of Zia ul Haq from securing enhanced military supplies from China. They have continued up to the present, and the signing of an agreement on nuclear cooperation between China and Pakistan in 1986 increased India's fears about Pakistan's long-term intentions.

It was such arms transfers that led many in India to give credence to the kind of view expressed by Girilal Jain, long-standing editor of the *Times of India*, when he asserted:

India has been apprehensive for a long time, certainly since the mid-sixties, that China looks upon Pakistan as a proxy for creating problems in India. China wants to deny us what we regard as our legitimate place in the sub-Himalayan region at least, if not in the larger region which could include the Gulf. As I see it, and as I think Indira Gandhi saw it, the problem with China is not mainly the border dispute, it's China's perception of India's role in South Asia.[3]

Thus whereas in the 1950s and 1960s India's response to Pakistan's arms purchases was to match capabilities, Thomas argues, 'from the mid 1970s a shift in India's defence strategy took place from one of "sufficient defence" to thwart Pakistani and Chinese attacks to one of "limited deterrence", implying a broadly based conventional and, if necessary, nuclear weapons capability'.[4] In return, the great increase in India's own arms industry, facilitated by Mrs Gandhi's arms agreements with the Soviet Union,[5] was seen in Pakistan as taking India further from non-alignment into the Soviet camp. Not surprisingly, the most important bilateral *casus belli* between India and Pakistan since Independence, the Kashmir question, remained unresolved.

Mrs Gandhi's declaration of a state of emergency in 1975 gained support from the Soviet Union, further strengthening the ties between the two governments. The movement towards the Soviet Union was not without opposition from within India, and Mrs Gandhi's defeat at the hands of the Janata Party in 1977 was followed by the declaration from Morarji Desai, India's new prime minister, that India would return to a position of absolute non-alignment.

The Janata period
Peter Lyon has suggested that the professed aim of the Janata government opened up three possibilities: an improvement in Indo-American relations, better links within the Commonwealth, and more constructive relationships with neighbouring countries. The increasing closeness between India and the Soviet Union had been a

cause of concern to Pakistan, which saw Soviet and Indian interests as a potentially powerful destabilizing force acting on Pakistan. Initially, therefore, Morarji Desai's declaration was welcome to Pakistan and the new military government of General Zia ul Haq, who viewed the strengthening of India's links with the Soviet Union as militating strongly against regional detente. Furthermore, as the Janata government took new initiatives towards China, the prospect was opened of a far wider regional detente even than had seemed possible under the terms of the Simla Accord.

The Janata government's initiative towards China fell foul of the Chinese war with Vietnam and Vietnam's invasion of Cambodia. However, it rapidly became apparent that Morarji Desai's government was not going to make a fundamental change in the direction of India's other major international ties. Overtures to the United States were more than matched by renewed commitments to the Soviet Union. India's refusal to sign the Non-Proliferation Treaty and the reluctance of the United States to continue to supply heavy water for the Tarapur reactor soured relations, despite assertions on both sides that the time was right for a new and positive relationship. In the event the mutual interests between India and the United States never became sufficiently strong during the Janata government's period in office to change the fundamental policy orientations of either. During those two and a half years the Janata government actively strengthened economic and military trading ties with the Soviet Union. Then the Soviet invasion of Afghanistan in December 1979 and the Western response to that invasion, far from providing necessary external support for a permanent settlement, doomed India and Pakistan to a further decade of sterile confrontation and escalating rearmament.

Afghanistan and after

The newly re-elected government of Mrs Gandhi, which took office within days of the Soviet occupation of Afghanistan, was immediately forced to take a position on the Soviet move. In the power vacuum between governments India's first response in the United Nations was written by the strongly pro-Soviet former Indian ambassador to Moscow, T.N. Kaul. Some saw in India's refusal to issue a simple condemnation of the Soviet invasion a sign that the Indian government had lost the independence of action that non-alignment was supposed to give.[6]

In fact from the end of January 1980 Mrs Gandhi clearly expressed her disapproval of the Soviet occupation. She and her foreign minister, P. V. Narasimha Rao, argued that the Soviet occupation threatened regional stability, and they tried to persuade Pakistan to agree not to escalate the regional arms race in response to the Soviet presence. Official visits between Soviet and Indian leaders to New Delhi in 1980 were notably cool, and a meeting between Mr Gromyko and Mrs Gandhi actually failed to produce a joint communiqué. In early 1980 and again in May 1987 the US government considered trying to persuade India to act as a mediator in order to achieve a Soviet withdrawal. This suggested that the US administration recognized that India was far from committed to the Soviet position. Yet the strategic importance to India of its friendship with the Soviet Union put it in a very delicate position. That delicacy was substantially increased by India's justified fear that the Soviet action would destabilize the region further by encouraging the United States to increase arms supplies to Pakistan.

It would be misleading to suggest that the immediate and adverse effect on India's relations with Pakistan was simply the inevitable result of superpower rivalries arriving on the South Asian doorstep. Between 1982 and 1984 Mrs Gandhi and Rajiv Gandhi, who had just stepped into his late brother's shoes as Mrs Gandhi's chosen political heir, used the purported threat of Pakistani aggression as a means of mustering support for the Congress Party in states such as Kashmir where its vote was seriously threatened by regional parties. Claims that Pakistan was preparing to attack India, which featured in the political rhetoric of Congress leaders, may have been designed for a domestic audience, but they scarcely suggested that improving relations with Pakistan was a top government priority.

Whatever the domestic political imperatives, there were objective reasons for India's growing concern over Pakistan's rearmament after 1979. These remained at the forefront of India's perceptions until the death of President Zia ul Haq in 1988. The 1987 official survey of India's foreign relations highlighted five reasons for the delay in normalizing relations with Pakistan following President Zia's visit of 17 December 1985: Pakistan's unwillingness to have non-discriminatory trade with India; the help which India believed that Pakistan was giving to Sikh terrorists; Pakistan's nuclear programme; Pakistan's keenness to acquire sophisticated weaponry such as AWACS; and finally, Pakistan's wish to 'internationalize' the Kashmir dispute in breach of the Simla Accord.

As General A.S. Vaidya put it in November 1985: 'Pakistan continues to be our principal security concern. Its acquisition of highly sophisticated weaponry, including the F-16s, battlefield surveillance aircraft and early warning systems have helped Pakistan take a quantum jump in arsenal and given it an offensive capability which we have to take note of.' He went on to argue that India's apparent numerical superiority in armed forces had to be seen in the light of its wider defence commitments. Thus although India remains committed, in the words of the annual Indian Foreign Office report, 'to developing cordial co-operative and good neighbourly relations with Pakistan in accordance with the letter and spirit of the Simla agreement', Pakistan's rearmament on the back of the Soviet occupation of Afghanistan continued to be seen as a challenge to India's vital security interests.

In such a context the spasmodic attempts to reach a permanent accommodation through mechanisms such as a no-war pact, first mooted by President Zia ul Haq in mid-September 1981, were doomed to fail. V. P. Dutt expressed Indian fears when he wrote that

the US strategy hampered the process of normalization between India and Pakistan and it introduced new levels of weapons in the regions ... India believed that its fears were confirmed by the fact that the bulk of Pakistan's troops were not on the borders of Afghanistan but on the borders of India. Only two of its seventeen divisions were reportedly on the Afghan border. Against such a background, discussion of Treaties of Friendship or No-War Pacts or no-first-use agreements was always seen more as a political gimmick than as a serious basis for establishing peace.[7]

Alongside the strengthening of Pakistan's conventional defences, the determined attempts by the Pakistani government to develop a nuclear weapons capability placed additional strain on India's security environment.

India has played its own nuclear hand with equal determination. Since its underground nuclear explosion in the Rajasthan desert in 1974 it has been clear that India was within reach of rapidly developing its own nuclear capability. SIPRI reported in 1988:

> ... evidence has accumulated in the past few years that both
> countries possess all the essential elements for the manufacture
> of nuclear weapons ... Pakistan is producing highly enriched,
> weapon grade uranium, and is probably testing a high-explosive
> 'triggering package' for a nuclear device ... India has greatly
> increased its plutonium production capacity in unsafeguarded
> facilities; it is considered by some experts to be capable of
> producing about 15 nuclear weapons per year.[8]

Given China's nuclear forces to the north, both Congress and Janata
governments consistently refused to sign the Nuclear Non-Proliferation
Treaty, keeping their nuclear options open.

To date the opponents of a nuclear defence strategy for India have
won the argument. Rajiv Gandhi remained a committed opponent
of developing a nuclear defensive strategy, and it is striking that the
perceived nuclear threat from China was insufficient to persuade
India to take advantage of the capability to make nuclear weapons
that it claims to have had since 1974. Nevertheless, public statements
such as the letter from India's First Secretary at the Embassy in
Washington to the *Washington Post* on 5 September 1987 made it
clear that nuclear development in Pakistan would be viewed dif-
ferently.

The argument over nuclear policy within India remains open. In
the new global context of superpower detente, informed Indian
circles expect the Soviet Union to put increasing pressure on the
Indian government to sign the NPT. It seems unlikely, however, that
V.P. Singh's government will make any abrupt change in policy,
since it hopes in the short term at least that improved relations with
Pakistan may make it possible to downgrade the nuclear question.

As for conventional weapons, in the mid-1980s India rapidly
increased its defence expenditure and widened its range of domesti-
cally produced defence equipment. In addition to the new arms deals
in such equipment as the Jaguar planes, India tested its first surface-
to-surface missile in March 1988, and its first ICBM launcher in
May 1989, the Agni rocket, part of a ten-year Integrated Guided
Missile Development Programme launched in June 1983.

The increased expenditure which these programmes entailed was
justified by the expansion of India's security interests and by the
heightened challenge to those interests in South Asia. Mutual fear
and distrust has run through all the key aspects of the relationship

between India and Pakistan during the 1980s. How else could the very high cost of the five-year campaign on the remote Siachen glacier, in the undemarcated territory between Indian- and Pakistani-held Kashmir, be understood? Although it is of very limited strategic importance to either India or Pakistan, since 1984 both sides have been more prepared to devote manpower and resources to defending literally useless territory than to achieving a political solution that is apparently too complex to be attainable.

Another running sore was the Indian fear that Pakistan was providing support for Sikh extremists across the Punjab border. As late as 23 February 1987 President Giani Zail Singh accused Pakistan of 'supporting anti-national groups in Punjab'.[9]

The political climate allowed some in the armed services to influence important aspects of regional foreign policy. Thus, India's massive demonstration of army power in its exercise Operation Brass Tacks at the end of 1986 (which, according to one authority, was the largest surface military operation in the world since World War II)[10] was taken under the guidance of the then Army Chief of Staff, General Sundarji, without India's political leaders apparently being aware of the scale of exercises involved or the threat that they would be seen as posing to Pakistan's security.

Similarly, the expansion of India's military hardware may owe as much to the demands of the separate services and to inter-service rivalry as to strategic planning from the Ministry of Defence or the Ministry of Foreign Affairs. Some authorities are severely critical of the Indian navy's procurement policies in the 1980s. Ashley Tellis has argued, for example, that 'in Indian defence debates the instruments of power excite greater controversy than their application'. He argued that 'no articulated strategy exists for naval operations', and he described two aircraft carriers bought from Britain, the Vikrant and the Virat, as 'pathetic assets', which would tie down one-third of the Indian navy simply to protect them, with no utility against any possible superpower presence in the Indian Ocean, nor against a now highly sophisticated Pakistani defence capability.[11] India's justification for further expansion of its naval strength, notably through the moves towards acquiring nuclear-powered submarines, rests on fears of Chinese intentions and potential capabilities, though it is questionable whether China will be other than a land-based power in the foreseeable future, despite the expansion of its own naval strength.

In an atmosphere of fear and suspicion, the demand for military expansion may seem politically justified despite crippling economic costs. The major question facing Indian policy-makers today is whether the removal of Soviet troops from Afghanistan at the end of February 1988, followed by the death of President Zia ul Haq and the election of a democratic government, has so changed the regional security environment that India and Pakistan can develop a relationship of mutual benefit rather than of mutually destructive military competition. The costs of failure to do so will be high. India's defence expenditure rose sharply between 1984–5 and 1987–8 from 16% of total government expenditure to over 19%. Financial stringency encouraged the government to impose cutbacks in 1988, but the new government responded to the political pressure of the Kashmir crisis by increasing the defence budget again in 1990.

Before the Kashmir crisis flared again agreements had already been reached on a mutual pact not to strike at each other's nuclear installations. Progress had also been reported in the bilateral talks on the Siachen glacier dispute, and both Pakistan and India had declared their determination not to allow disaffected groups, whether from Punjab or Sind, to use each other's territory as bases for training and support. Such steps towards regional detente have been blocked by the Kashmir dispute.

No resolution is in sight. Pakistan remains deeply concerned over India's use and control of the Indus tributaries, an issue with vital security and economic considerations, especially for Pakistan. It will need extremely sensitive handling on both sides, and neither the Indian nor the Pakistani governments have much domestic political room for manoeuvre.

Afghanistan also remained a particularly sensitive issue, but the Indian government was convinced at the end of 1989 that Prime Minister Bhutto wished to find a political solution rather than the military one which has favoured Islamic fundamentalist mujahidin groups and which had enjoyed the powerful backing of the previous Pakistani government and of the United States.[12] Further complications arise over the attitudes of the superpowers to the Afghan conflict. India's crucial interest is the maintenance of a non-fundamentalist government in Afghanistan. The support of the US administration and its allies, at least until mid-1990, for the continuing military push by the Afghan guerrillas against the Najibullah government was seen by India as diametrically opposed to that interest. The failure of the guerrillas to topple the Najibullah government in the coup attempt of January 1990 helped to strengthen Prime Minister Benazir Bhutto's hand in her own efforts to achieve domestic support for a political solution. Such a solution, however, remains far off.

There can be no doubt that the Soviet withdrawal from Afghanistan and the much more far-reaching changes in Soviet foreign policy itself have fundamental implications for India's relations with Pakistan and its entire region. On successive high-profile visits to New Delhi, Gorbachev has made clear his wish that all the countries of Asia should greatly improve their relations. Senior Indian politicians and officials recognize that there is no longer the powerful coincidence of strategic interests between India and the Soviet Union that characterized the period between 1968 and 1986. While India may well remain a key piece in Soviet strategy in Asia, the Non-Aligned Movement and the developing world, it can no longer expect to enjoy the unique leverage which brought it such significant political and economic benefits for two decades.

The government of Rajiv Gandhi was sympathetic to the problems of Prime Minister Bhutto's fledgling democratic government. When it took power the Singh government talked of improving relations with Pakistan. The weakness of Benazir Bhutto's government and the uncertain future of India's ruling coalition, together with the crisis in Kashmir, leave the potential gains of the new geopolitical situation still a long way from realization.

India and Sri Lanka

Whereas the adversarial relationship between India and Pakistan dates from Independence, Sri Lanka and India have enjoyed long periods of comparative cordiality. Not that there were no conflicts of interest between the two governments. The denial of citizenship to estate workers of Indian Tamil origin in 1948 left nearly one million Tamil workers stateless. The Ceylon Citizenship Act of 1948 was followed by the Indian and Pakistani Residents (Citizenship) Act of 1949. The effect, as Farmer has pointed out, was 'effectively to deny citizenship to the vast majority of Indian Tamils'.[13]

The denial of citizenship was regarded as offensive by many in India, and the government sought to work for a solution to the problem by negotiation. In 1964 Mr Shastri, then India's prime minister, had successfully concluded a deal which was widely seen in India as generous to Sri Lanka. Under this agreement, subsequently confirmed and strengthened by Mrs Gandhi and Mrs Bandaranaike, over 750,000 Tamil plantation workers were to be repatriated to India, the remainder being granted Sri Lankan citizenship.

India's willingness to accept such terms despite the considerable problems that repatriation posed, particularly in Tamil Nadu, reflected the government's humanitarian concern for the 'Indian Tamils' and the strategic assessment of the greater value that would accrue to India by keeping good government-to-government relations with Sri Lanka. Unlike Pakistan, Sri Lanka never posed a direct military threat to India. Furthermore, under Mrs Bandaranaike's Sri Lanka Freedom Party (SLFP) government the evidence of rising ethnic chauvinism (which has dominated the island's politics during the last decade) was recognized in New Delhi but seen as an internal problem for Sri Lanka which called for no direct involvement by India. Indeed, the close relationship forged by Mrs Gandhi and Mrs Bandaranaike, together with the latter's determination to keep Western influence in the Indian Ocean at a minimum, formed the basis for firm political cooperation.

Indian-Sri Lankan relations, however, continued to oscillate. After the anti-Tamil pogrom of July 1983 they were marked by a deepenening nervous distrust on both sides. The 1978 election victory of the UNP under President Jayawardene had already contributed to this deterioration. The new Sri Lankan government swept aside the socialist policies of the previous government and set about liberalizing the island's economy. At the same time it pursued a foreign policy which was seen in India as tilting sharply towards the West. Coupled with the ending of the close personal relationship which had existed between the Sri Lankan and Indian prime ministers, the changes meant a significant distancing between the two governments.

In themselves, however, these changes did not necessarily imply an inevitable breakdown in the long-term ties between the two. There were no inherent conflicts of interest to divide them, and while some of the Buddhist Sinhalese had seen themselves as potentially threatened by the mass of Hindu India to the north, represented within Sri Lanka in their eyes by the Jaffna Tamils, the Indian commitment to non-interference in Sri Lanka's internal affairs and India's agreement over the tea plantation workers had suggested that an amicable relationship could continue indefinitely. The rise of competitive chauvinism in Sri Lanka's domestic politics, directed fiercely against the indigenous Tamil population rather than against the 'Indian' Tamils changed that radically in the 1980s.[14]

Between 1980 and 1983 successive moves by the Sri Lankan government had destroyed the political credibility of moderate Tamil political opinion. By then such opinion was represented by the Tamil United Liberation Front. In the late 1970s the TULF was regarded as an extreme Tamil movement, but several groups rose in their place with the objective of complete independence for a Tamil state in the north and the east of the island, an independence which could be achieved only through violence. In the space of a few months after 1982 the Liberation Tigers of Tamil Eelam (the LTTE or Tamil Tigers) had staked out a claim to widespread support through a succession of violent acts, as had a number of other groups of varying ideological persuasions. Where the moderates of the TULF had failed to deliver, the Tigers began to show that they could seriously worry the government.

The massacre of Tamils which took place in Colombo at the end of July 1983, in reprisal for an ambush by Tamil Tigers in which thirteen Sinhalese soldiers were killed, led to a crisis that immediately involved India in the Sri Lankan domestic situation. Some 130,000 refugees fled from Sri Lanka to Tamil Nadu, increasing steadily to over 160,000. The government provided camps for them in Tamil Nadu. It was widely believed in Sri Lanka that such camps were terrorist training camps. As a leading member of the SLFP told me in May 1987, 'there are training camps right throughout India – Assam, Delhi, Punjab – and into these camps Tamils went, probably without the Central Government's deliberate planning'. In May 1987 A.P. Venkateshwaran, who had recently left the post of India's Foreign Secretary, stated to me that although it was impossible to guarantee that no training went on in the refugee camps, he believed there was no support given to it by the Indian government. However, some responsible Indian journalists clearly disagreed. Pran Chopra, a noted Indian political commentator, wrote in May 1987 that 'India's failure in the recent past, and it is very serious, has been that it has not sufficiently tried to use its leverage with the

Tamil militants for bringing them to the negotiating table. It has not applied such pressure upon them, as it could have, which would have made it irresistible.'[15]

The deteriorating situation in Sri Lanka, however, posed extra problems for India. They were met during the next three years by a government response full of uncertainties and contradictions. The stories of atrocities against the Tamils had an immediate effect in Tamil Nadu. Despite the common cultural heritage, in many respects there had been little affinity between the Tamils of Jaffna and those of India before 1983. However, the scale of the disaster taking place across the narrow Palk Straits roused strong sympathies and demands from all strands of Tamil political opinion to support the Tamil cause.

The Indian government had always stood on the principle of non-interference, but that had not prevented Mrs Gandhi from making it very clear when she believed that Indian interests were in danger of being compromised. In practice the government operated from two basic premises. The first was that it could not support secessionist demands in any way, and the second was that it could not tolerate the large-scale killing of Tamils. While Mrs Gandhi recognized that the ethnic problem was a national question for Sri Lanka, she also stressed India's interest in the question of displaced Tamils, stateless tea plantation workers, and the importance of Sri Lanka's geographical proximity to India. Pran Chopra observed of India's policy during 1983 and 1984 that 'India's record was nothing much to be proud of'. He cited a number of failings, the most important of which was that India 'seriously and cynically meddled in the conflict through turning the other way'.[16]

Rajiv Gandhi came to power at the end of 1984. He was anxious to follow different tactics in relations with India's neighbours from those that had been the hallmark of his mother's rule. Where she had used direct pressure and strong hints of direct involvement, he offered reasoned discussion on a basis of supposed equality. But despite his exuberant air, suggesting a belief that all regional problems could be resolved by sensible talking carried out at the highest levels of government, he showed little interest in the details of the regional problem that lay at the heart of the Sri Lankan crisis.

Within the Foreign Affairs Ministry he downgraded the role of G. Parthasarathy, one of the chief experts on the Sri Lankan Tamil question. According to highly placed sources, in May 1985 he charged his newly appointed Foreign Secretary, Romesh Bhandari, with the task of 'sorting out the Sri Lanka crisis in thirty days'. *India Today*'s description of Romesh Bhandari's early days as Foreign Secretary is noteworthy: 'In striking contrast to his predecessor, the ascetic, aloof and Brahmanical G.P. Parthasarathy, Bhandari arrived in Colombo bursting with bonhomie and succeeded in winning official approval in Colombo. He has earned the nickname "no problem" Bhandari and the hurriedly convened Rajiv-Jayawardene summit was partly the result of his efforts.'[17] But many in Tamil Nadu believed that in making the change Rajiv Gandhi was handing responsibility to someone with neither the personal knowledge nor the temperament to argue the subtleties of either the Sri Lankan Tamil or the Indian Tamil positions.

In part the reasons for this appointment may be traced to the anxiety of the new prime minister to achieve quick and dramatic results both in domestic and foreign policy. In addition New Delhi feared that Sri Lanka was increasingly in danger of moving from its position of friendly neutrality towards India into the camp of Western military alliances. The view was forcefully expressed by Praful Bidwai, a columnist in the *Times of India*,[18] who argued that from 1985 Indian policy was deliberately weakening India's interests in Sri Lanka in favour of those of the United States and other Western powers – evidenced, he claimed, by the decision of the government of Sri Lanka to allow large new transmitters for the Voice of America and by the attractiveness of the port of Trincomalee to US interests. There is no evidence at all to suggest that in the 1980s such arguments had any weight in the United States, or that it had shown any interest in using Trincomalee, but that view had some currency in New Delhi.

Such strategic perceptions illustrate the extent to which even the shadow of superpower influence in the region has been a potent influence on Indian foreign policy thinking. But while the annexure to the Indo-Sri Lankan Accord certainly bears out that interpretation of India's motivations for getting directly involved in Sri Lanka's crisis, there is every reason to believe that the conditions imposed on the Sri Lankan government were almost an afterthought, designed to make the Indian action more acceptable to the domestic political audience. As the Indian government attempted to sponsor solution after solution, from the Thimpu meeting of SAARC through to the November 1986 meeting in Bangalore, the evidence suggests that policy was a response to day-to-day events and a wish to find 'a solution' rather than the clear-sighted pursuit of well-defined goals by means that were within India's control.

Events in Sri Lanka consistently failed to respond to India's wish that they would fall into place without direct interference from India. It proved easier to talk of the principles of mutual non-interference in the internal affairs of one's neighbours than to practise it in the presence of 160,000 Tamil refugees. A solution had to be found which would be acceptable both to Tamil opinion in Sri Lanka and to Tamil sensitivities in India, neither of which had had any previous influence on India's dealings with its neighbours. Even in November 1986 at the time of the SAARC meeting in Bangalore, when Rajiv Gandhi accepted President Jayawardene's 'trifurcation' proposals for the north and east of Sri Lanka, it seemed that the Indian government preferred to keep the Tamils at arm's length.

India was anxious to sustain the traditional official policy of no direct interference in its neighbours' internal affairs. It wanted nothing to do with any secessionist political movement, and it was also conscious of the parallel which the Sri Lankan government stressed between the violent activities of the movement for Tamil Eelam in Sri Lanka and the terrorism in Punjab. Not surprisingly the conflicting pressures contributed to the government's difficulties in steering a consistent path and provoked strident criticism.[19]

All of this prevented a quick solution. One reason lay in the fact that the Indian government made no effort to establish the nature of the Sri Lankan Tamils' demands as a basis for mediation and negotiation. Crucial to these were three issues: the contiguity of the northern and eastern regions of Tamil settlement in Sri Lanka, the control of land rights, and the devolution of legislative as well as executive power to the Tamil region. Failure to achieve effective mediation rapidly compounded India's difficulties, not to say those of the Tamils in Sri Lanka itself.

To the Sri Lankan government, the willingness of India to give a home to the leaders of the Tamil Tigers signified the Indian government's compromised position and determination to enforce a solution that suited India's purpose. Yet the Tigers themselves felt completely cold-shouldered by the government in Delhi, depending on the state government and in particular on the Chief Minister, M.G. Ramachandran, for both moral and practical support. It is striking that Vellupillai Prabhakaran, the leader of the Tigers, claimed to the assistant editor of *The Hindu* to have three personal heroes: M.G. Ramachandran, Netaji Subhas Chandra Bose (the Indian nationalist founder of the Indian National Army) and Mahatma Gandhi. Yet despite the close personal ties between the then Chief Minister of Tamil Nadu and Prabhakaran, political tension in South India during 1985 and 1986 prevented anything like total support for the Sri Lankan Tamil cause, and there was rising resentment in Tamil Nadu over the behaviour of some of the militant groups in Madras.

A second and equally potent factor, in the view of a former Indian foreign secretary, may have been the fact that the government of India during this period was sending the wrong signals to the government of Sri Lanka, implying that it was in India's interest to be asked to mediate, rather than in the Sri Lankan interest. While that analysis is controversial, the difficulties facing the Indian government were undoubtedly made still more severe by actions of the government of Sri Lanka, which by 1985 and 1986 was deeply embedded in the competitive chauvinism of Sinhalese political interests. The government encouraged an active Sinhalese colonization programme in areas claimed by the Tamils as regions in which previously they had been predominant. At the same time the Sri Lankan government stepped up its military attacks, imposing an economic blockade on Jaffna and moving the army in a concerted assault in May 1987.

That marked a point of no return for Indian policy on Sri Lanka. Preoccupied as it had been with problems in Punjab and on its borders with Pakistan, the Indian government was forced to turn its full attention to the Sri Lankan crisis and to abandon its apparently distant stance of non-interference. First an attempt was made to break the economic blockade by an abortive shipment of food aid across the Palk Straits. When this ended in a fiasco, the Indian air force organized an airlift. At the end of July, Rajiv Gandhi flew to Colombo to meet President Jayawardene. On 29 July, four years to the day after the worst of the riots and atrocities in Colombo, an Accord was signed. An Indian Peace-Keeping Force was to be established in the north and east of Sri Lanka and was to take over policing duties, supervising the surrender of arms by the Tamil Tigers and preparing the ground for a return to democratic elections, for which provisions were also made.

In itself the Sri Lankan government was not breaking new ground in signing an Accord seeking the help of India. Nepal, Bangladesh and Sri Lanka had all called on India's assistance previously. However, the Accord had an annexure attached in the form of an exchange of letters, specifying India's insistence on a Sri Lankan guarantee that no military use would be made by any outside power of either port or broadcasting facilities. In exchange for this undertaking India agreed *inter alia* to deport any Sri Lankan national 'found to be engaging in terrorist activities or advocating separatism or secessionism'.

The Accord was greeted with relief and satisfaction in India, though its reception in Sri Lanka was far less favourable. Some Sinhalese feared a sell-out to Indian pressure and it was strongly opposed in the Sri Lankan cabinet by the then prime minister, Ranasinghe Premadasa. Furthermore the Indian Peace-Keeping Force found it impossible to prevent the Tamil Tigers from continuing to take violent action, notably in the eastern province. From the outset it was clear that there was no long-term 'game plan' when the Indian troops went in, and there remained little evidence of strategic thinking throughout. In the first few weeks of the Accord the Peace-Keeping Force was the last thin protection against an ethnic catastrophe on an unprecedented scale. That remained its best justification, but failure to achieve a rapid solution increasingly opened the IPKF to accusations of being an unwelcome occupying force. By the end of 1988 over 700 Indian soldiers had been killed,[20] mainly by the Tamil guerrillas of the LTTE, whom the Peace-Keeping Force had been intended to disarm.

Neither the holding of elections for provincial councils nor the election of Ranasinghe Premadasa as President in the election of 19 December 1988 brought any respite to the deepening domestic political chaos. As a move to quell the rapid escalation of politically motivated violence throughout the island, President Premadasa demanded the withdrawal of the Indian Peace-Keeping Force by the second anniversary of the Accord.

It looked like a desperate throw. Even though ultimately an agreement on withdrawal was reached, the chances of it resulting in long-term political stability seemed slight. The Indian government showed continuing uncertainty as to how to act, and it was left to the new government of V.P. Singh to complete the withdrawal in March 1990.

For India, calculation of the political costs remains premature. With no obvious success to be laid at the IPKF's door, withdrawal may ease the immediate financial and military burden without offering any improvement in India's long-term interest. Since the 1983 pogrom India's incoherent steps towards greater involvement in Sri Lanka's affairs were aimed at avoiding the political chaos in that country which it feared would have dire implications for its own domestic future. But far from being welcomed as liberating heroes, the role that had been so politically successful in India's assistance to Bangladesh in 1971, the Indian army was bogged down in a bitter war of occupation. Perhaps not surprisingly, the relief of 29 July 1987 had turned to frustration and a feeling of good riddance by March 1990. In Tamil Nadu itself the general election campaign of November 1989 paid scant attention to Sri Lanka, and there was a widespread wish that the problem would simply go away. Meanwhile the chaos the Accord was designed to prevent still looms as large as ever. In June 1990 the fragile peace between the Tamil Tigers and the Sri Lankan government collapsed, and fierce fighting broke out once more. It would be rash to underestimate the implications for Tamil Nadu and for India of a renewed Sri Lankan government offensive against Jaffna.

India and China

If India's South Asian pre-eminence was ensured by the break-up of Pakistan and the creation of Bangladesh in 1971, its status on the wider regional front was far more equivocal. Nancy Jetly writes that 'Sino-Indian relations are thus shaped not only by considerations of mutual status and role, but also by the larger factors of regional and global polity'.[21] China's bitter hostility to India's links with the Soviet Union has been matched by a determination to develop strong friendships with Pakistan, Bangladesh, Nepal and Sri Lanka. From the Indian viewpoint these were viewed as both potentially and actually destabilizing.

Gorbachev's reorientation of Soviet foreign policy towards Asia and the wider relationships between the superpowers have profound long-term implications for Indian and Chinese relations. Yet the border question remains the crucial factor in Sino-Indian normalization.

India and China share over 4000 kilometres of border.[22] It runs

77

through territory that Sir Thomas Holditch, Surveyor General of India at the end of the nineteenth century, described as 'the finest natural combination of boundary and barrier that exists in the world'. Yet its remote, dramatic and inaccessible nature has not prevented the frontier region being strongly contested. Dorothy Woodman argued that 'the Himalayas have dominated the Asian policy of Britain, China and Russia. And since geographical factors remain to a large extent constant, they still determine the shape of policy adopted by China, India, Pakistan and the Soviet Union as well as that of the smaller states which are on the Himalayan periphery.'[23]

The contest between India and China reflects sharply contrasting interests in the region. For China the Aksai Chin and the Karakoram in the western Himalayas are a strategically important link to the westernmost Chinese province of Xinjiang. The high-altitude, barren plateau region provides a vital land route, and the completion of the strategic road across it between 1954 and 1957 gave China its only reliable link for military supplies to its western borders with the Soviet Union.

For India's part Nehru saw the issue of the entire Himalayan border, not just the Aksai Chin in the west but also the eastern borderlands of what is now Arunachal Pradesh, as a territorial question settled by the treaties under which the McMahon Line was agreed in 1914. Alastair Lamb suggests that in the Sino-Indian Agreement of 1954, in which India recognized China's sovereignty over Tibet, Nehru 'did not seem to realise the full implications of what he had done. He believed that pious phrases about the five principles of peaceful co-existence and the general atmosphere of Asian anti-imperialist solidarity would make the Chinese, without protest, accept an Indian-dictated boundary alignment'.[24]

As far as the Chinese were concerned, however, no boundary agreement had ever been reached. They did not accept the McMahon Line in the east, which had been agreed by Tibet in the 1914 treaty. This followed broadly the Himalayan crest watershed line, while the Chinese claimed that the frontier lay along the foot of the Assam hills. Equally the Chinese had never signed any agreements on the Tibetan borders in the west.

In recognizing Chinese sovereignty over Tibet, India went some of the way towards reversing the British policy of keeping a buffer zone between China and India and accepting China as a direct neighbour.

It was clearly not far enough. The Chinese may have wished to use the 1962 dispute to demonstrate 'India's military feet of clay' and to bring pressure on India to recognize Chinese rights in the Aksai Chin, which it saw as a vital strategic interest.[25] But the war was at least in part caused by India's failure to recognize that the boundary inherited from the colonial period would have to be renegotiated directly with the Chinese if it were to cease to be a constant source of dispute.

The immediate result of the war was the withdrawal of India's ambassador from Beijing and of China's ambassador from New Delhi. The Indian government decided to re-examine its policy towards China in 1969, when India offered to hold talks without any preconditions, but no ambassador returned until 1976.[26]

In practice, definition of the boundary on the ground is impossible simply by reference to the McMahon Line itself. As a former Indian foreign secretary and ambassador to China put it, the dispute over the border 'is partly a dispute over what the McMahon Line means'. While the text accompanying McMahon's definition specifies the 'high crest watershed of the Himalayas' as the boundary, his maps are sometimes vague and inaccurate, including mountain ranges, valleys and villages that do not exist, and omitting some that do.

Not surprisingly this has left ample scope for disagreement on the ground. Such disagreements have flared spasmodically since the 1962 war. The Indian position after this war was made more difficult by Nehru's assertions of India's absolute and non-negotiable rights to all the land included in 'British' India. Neville Maxwell claims that Nehru rejected a status quo solution to the border dispute in 1962 on the grounds that 'if I give them that, I shall no longer be Prime Minister of India. I will not do it.'[27] Certainly India's defeat in 1962 raised the domestic political stakes for any government that might subsequently seek a solution through negotiating over territory.

It also made the possibility of doing a deal on some form of 'territorial exchange' politically explosive in India – such as agreeing the exchange of the Aksai Chin in the western sector for Arunachal Pradesh in the east (long advocated by Zhou Enlai in the 1950s, and the basis of the Chinese negotiating position in the early 1980s).

Although tension eased after 1976, and although there was no evidence to suggest that either side had any interest in renewed conflict in the 1980s, there was also little to suggest that the domestic

79

political benefits of a settlement were seen in India as sufficient to make the compromises that would have been essential to the permanent delimitation of these boundaries. India took the initiative in the early 1980s in trying to achieve agreement, but progress remained extremely slow, and the sixth round of talks in November 1985 'only confirmed existing divergences in approach'.[28]

The domestic complications in moving towards accommodation with China are suggested by the opposition from Rajiv Gandhi's own Foreign Ministry to his visit to Beijing from 19 to 22 December 1988. However, it is clear that India's view of its relationship with China and of the border question is now fundamentally different from that of 1962. India recognizes that it has to come to terms with China as its immediate neighbour. It is sensitive to the scale of China's regional power, and to its capacity to cause major problems within the South Asian region, for example through military assistance to Pakistan, possible help for Pakistan's nuclear programme, and the upgrading of the Karakoram Highway, giving enhanced access to the north-western region of South Asia.[29] For well over ten years India has avoided taking action which could antagonize China unnecessarily, though at the same time it has built up its defence capabilities to make sure that the 1962 military débâcle is not repeated.

Fears of such an encounter have largely disappeared. Leading Indian officials believe that Indian defences are now sufficiently strong to guarantee that there will be no Chinese invasion of the plains. At the same time there can be no question of India posing an aggressive threat to China by any advance over the high ranges. In this light even China's nuclear capability is not seen as a real threat, for current strategic thinking in the Indian government believes that any significant military action would still have to be based on conventional forces.

The Indian government has believed for some time that force is not going to change the relationship between China and India. It is true that the 1986 'threat' of Chinese military action after India granted full statehood to Arunachal Pradesh caused great embarrassment to the Indian government. The contemporary reports of the 'Chinese intrusion into the Sumdorong Chu valley in Arunachal Pradesh' and of a huge Chinese military build-up on the border[30] were subsequently shown to be completely false, and it is difficult to find any evidence that either side sees any advantage in conflict.

The official Indian view is that China has at least as great an interest as the Soviet Union, and for the same reasons, in reducing its military spending and in achieving stable political solutions to its outstanding problems with its neighbours. Although Chinese actions in Tibet cause concern in India, Rajiv Gandhi was firmly committed to pushing for a realistic resolution of the border question.

There is some evidence that Indian public opinion has shifted too. Passions no longer run as high as they did, and the public reception of Rajiv Gandhi's visit to China exceeded his private advisers' highest expectations. He believed at the end of 1989 that it would be possible to adopt a genuine negotiating position and that therefore border issues could be tackled. However, it is certain that although the process has been initiated it will take years rather than months to achieve mutually acceptable results.

Jetly's view that 'a stable peace between India and China would have to rest not only on a satisfactory resolution of the border dispute on agreed principles – necessarily involving some territorial give and take – but also on a clear recognition of their relative power status and geo-political stakes in the region' is widely accepted.[31] The favourable domestic response to Rajiv Gandhi's visit to Beijing in December 1988 suggested that the new Indian government may have more room to manoeuvre in its expressed desire to press for resolution of the boundary question than at any time since 1962. However, with both the Indian and the Chinese governments embattled, the prospects for progress have receded.

SAARC – a framework for regional co-operation?

Progress towards regional cooperation in South Asia has been as slow as that of Lord Jagganath's temple car in Puri's Rath Yatra. Given the nature and scale of bilateral problems between India and its neighbours, that is hardly surprising. Indeed, the very process of Partition which created the two states of India and Pakistan in 1947 and their subsequent separate political development inhibited any thought of significant cooperation between such apparently unequal partners. Immediately after Independence the economies of India and Pakistan moved even further apart and trade between them virtually ceased. This had particularly striking effects on West Bengal and East Pakistan, where the jute-producing regions of

Pakistan were cut off from the industrial processing belt of Calcutta in a deliberate attempt by the Pakistani government to protect infant industries in the previously unindustrialized East Bengal.

That action was symptomatic of the lack of economic integration within South Asia, and further militated against developing common regional institutions with shared political and economic goals. The South Asian Association for Regional Cooperation was first mooted by the then President of Bangladesh, Zia ur Rahman, in late 1979. It was launched in August 1983, though preparatory ministerial meetings had been held previously at Colombo in 1981, Islamabad in 1982 and Dhaka in 1983. It was formally inaugurated at Dhaka on 8 December 1985.

Yet trade within the South Asian region for the individual member countries of the newly created SAARC was extremely small. Bilateral trade between India and Pakistan was even smaller: at the time of the formal inception of SAARC in 1985 Pakistan's trade with India was considerably lower than with Bangladesh.

The very low level of intra-regional trade suggests not only the minimal extent of economic contact within the region but also the extent to which the regional economies are competitive rather than complementary. That problem is exacerbated by their imbalance. India's comparatively rapid industrial development gives it a competitive edge which is feared by its neighbours. But if they had been suspicious that India would dominate any regional economic organization, India under Mrs Gandhi's leadership had feared the political possibilities of six smaller nations using a common forum against Indian interests. Rajiv Gandhi determined to adopt a more cooperative approach, and the brain-child of President Zia ur Rahman developed into the first regional association only when India put its weight behind the concept. The movement to build institutions of regional cooperation was given immediate impetus by Rajiv Gandhi when he formed his new government in early 1985.

Even then the SAARC Charter, on Indian insistence, excluded consideration of contentious bilateral issues. India has now become a strong advocate and supporter of the movement. However, SAARC has yet to develop either a significant economic role or any political muscle. King Birendra of Nepal told SAARC foreign ministers attending their fourth conference, at Kathmandu in August 1988, that 'SAARC may not yet have become a palpable reality but it has certainly become a part of the reality of the hopes, faith and aspirations in the hearts and minds of the people of South Asia who seek peace, happiness and security with honour and dignity.'[32] The December 1988 summit failed to agree on the admission of Afghanistan to SAARC, and in mid-1990 a question mark hung over SAARC's future development, its viability still clearly contingent on the resolution of regional bilateral problems.

6
INDIA ON THE WORLD STAGE

In 1985 Appadorai and Rajan noted a fundamental paradox about Indian foreign policy.

> When it had a traditional image, India used to play (until the 1960s) a notable role in world affairs. Today India is known as a sleeping economic giant, the fourth largest military power (in conventional weapons), and the largest and most stable democracy in the world. The odd thing, however, is that, nowadays, India plays a much less active and important role in world affairs – for a variety of reasons, but especially because of the Government's preoccupation with acute domestic problems, and of the standing threat to India's security.[1]

Those problems have been real enough. However, on the wider stage, India's preoccupations have naturally included but gone beyond such concerns. While economic interests have played a negligible role in its South Asian regional policies, since 1971 they have played an ever-increasing part in its policies towards countries beyond.

In the post-colonial world it was inevitable that India's foreign ties would reflect its new status as well as new national perceptions. Superpower confrontation has been the linchpin of global political relations since World War II. The different South Asian governments have adapted to that reality according to their own position and interests, not just according to their ideologies and political stance, but also in relation to their geopolitical position within the superpower areas of rivalry. Although non-alignment has been a prominent feature of Indian policy since Independence and remains so today, and although India has played a significant role in multinational forums such as the United Nations, the Non-Aligned Movement and the Commonwealth, it has been unable to escape the pervasive influence of global superpower confrontation. Equally, none of these forums have been substitutes for bilateral means of pursuing political and economic interests.

Whereas India has had extremely close ties with the Soviet Union since 1971, its links with the United States have been subject to far greater strain. Peter Duncan's recent book has explored in depth the Soviet links with India. This chapter focuses more on the obstacles to close ties between India and the United States.

Non-alignment and superpower interests

In 1947 India saw itself as a natural leader for all those countries which were trying to follow its own path of peaceful coexistence. From the outset it took an active role in the United Nations and the Commonwealth, and it was a founder member of the Non-Aligned Movement in 1961.

The degree of commitment shown by India to each of these institutions might seem surprising to those who argue that they have proved powerless to shape international events or to move beyond the publication of bland statements of principle. Nor is it easy to identify direct benefits obtained by India from its membership of any of the institutions. Mrs Gandhi showed a much less pronounced attachment to the Commonwealth than either her father or her son, and it seemed sometimes as if she had to be actively persuaded to take part even in its major meetings.

Similarly, the stance taken by the United Nations on Kashmir in the 1950s was widely seen as hostile to India's interests, and Indian diplomacy failed to prevent a sharply critical response to its military takeover of the Portuguese colony of Goa in 1961. Indeed, Krishna Menon, Minister without Portfolio and later Defence Minister, when asked what India got out of the United Nations, responded 'nothing'.[2]

Nevertheless, to suggest that India's concern to play an active role in international forums since Independence has been entirely altruistic would be to miss the importance which international opinion moulded by those institutions may have for India's own freedom of action, both in its region and on a wider footing. Its adverse experience in bringing its bilateral dispute with Pakistan to the United Nations in January 1948 was widely seen in India as a reason not for downplaying its role but for improving its effectiveness in achieving its objectives. International approval for its action in the Maldives in 1988, which came from both the Commonwealth and the United Nations, is evidence of the political gains which have been achievable.

Yet purely regional objectives have never been the primary concern in India's participation in the United Nations. Mrs Vijayalakshmi Pandit, India's first ambassador to the United Nations, devoted her opening contribution to South Africa's treatment of its Indian residents. This symbolized the links between global concerns of human rights and racial equality, espoused by Gandhi and by the new Congress government of India, and the more restricted Indian interests overseas.

In fact India's growing participation in international forums has reflected two principles. First, as Nehru himself recognized, the United Nations and subsequently the Non-Aligned Movement gave expression to fundamental Indian beliefs in peaceful cooperation between nations, to decolonization and to the achievement of full independence through economic development as well as political freedom. India's deep hostility to the cold war outlook of the superpowers in the 1950s reflected both opposition in principle to that stance and fear as to its implications for India's own future and for that of other newly independent states. If the choice was between joining one of the superpower blocs or attempting to foster an alternative forum of international political cooperation, India had no doubt about the direction in which it wished to move.

The unattractiveness of the alternative certainly encouraged India to play a part in a forum where in any case it saw itself as having a degree of natural leadership. But Nehru was also persuaded to take India into the Commonwealth. In doing so India became the first republic to join. It also provided a bridge between the former colonial power and the newly decolonized countries, and between the developed and the developing world.

It is not a role that has always been easy to fulfil, and in a polarized world it sometimes carried diplomatic costs. At the heart of the triangular relationship between India, the Soviet Union and the United States lie sharply contrasting interpretations of India's non-aligned stance. India has always defined non-alignment in terms of securing its independence of action from either of the major power blocs and retaining freedom of international association and policy to act in accordance with its own basic interests. William Barnds suggested three other reasons for India's non-alignment policy:

1. The country's major tasks were the internal ones of political, social and economic development, on which it should concentrate rather than becoming involved in a struggle between the West and the communist powers that did not directly concern it. 2. Taking either side in the conflict would be divisive among a people badly in need of greater national unity, and 3. As the strongest power in the area, India had no need for external support to bolster its regional position.[3]

The bottom line has been a refusal to be drawn into alliances or defence pacts with either superpower that would restrict India's ultimate freedom of action.

At the outset the United States found that concept very difficult to come to terms with. As one American participant in a conference on India and the United States put it, 'the Indian concept of non-alignment is offensive to American values'. The United States has constantly sought alliances among Third World countries. In their absence it has seen either latent or active hostility to US interests. India's non-alignment was given a degree of acceptability by Eisenhower's interpretation of it as 'equidistance' between the superpowers, but to India the very concept of equidistance implies acceptance of the cold war power-bloc mentality which it has rejected on grounds both of principle and of national self-interest.

More recently, India's voting pattern in the United Nations was widely criticized by the Reagan administration. In 1987 the US ambassador to the United Nations, Vernon Walters, reported to the US Congress on voting patterns in the General Assembly. Amongst other things, he pointed to India's voting as often inimical to US interests. He highlighted a 'stark contrast' between states such as Israel, Japan and Western Europe, which voted with the United States on 90%, 69% and 66% of occasions respectively, and India, for which the figure was 10%. Although the selectivity of the issues chosen for comparisons of votes has been questioned, and although he ignored the fact that over half the decisions are taken by consensus, the American criticism of those not toeing the administration's line is noteworthy.

As to the Soviet Union, it is also true that in the early years Stalin found India's independent stance no easier. However, the Soviet Union's interest in stability and balance in South Asia, and its fear of seeing its South Asian neighbours enter hostile, Western-oriented encircling pacts encouraged a more ready acceptance of Indian non-alignment as a necessary price of friendship. From the mid-1950s the Soviet leaders were far more prepared to tolerate what Stalin had dismissed as India's petty bourgeois government and its non-aligned stance in exchange for the political benefits of a secured friendship. Yet India has shown a corresponding resistance to Soviet attempts to draw it into formal alliances, notably through the Brezhnev collective security proposals. In the 1950s and 1960s Soviet ambitions had been limited in this respect. As Duncan has argued, 'while the Americans encouraged countries to join security alliances, the aim of the USSR was to discourage them from doing this rather than entering formal alliances with itself'.[4] The Indo-Soviet Treaty of Friendship went well beyond the negative status of a non-aggression pact without in any sense tying India into a military alliance.

That position continued to hold after Gorbachev's visit to New Delhi in November 1986. The Soviet leader had raised again the possibility of an Asian collective security arrangement in his Vladivostok speech earlier in the year – a proposal which had received the warm approbation of T.N. Kaul, a long-term supporter of the Soviet Union and then Indian ambassador in Moscow. But the Indian government has remained obdurately opposed to any such scheme. In P.M. Kamath's view, 'if we separate the entire gamut of international relations into various segments like diplomatic, economic, educational, cultural and scientific elements, it is seen that India's tilt towards the Soviet Union is confined to the diplomatic realms. India heavily leans towards the US in other areas.'[5]

As was shown in Chapter 4, part of the reason for the strength of those ties with the Soviet Union is economic. Nevertheless, despite the importance of India's trade with the USSR, in economic terms the role of Eastern bloc countries is dwarfed by that of OECD countries, and is an inadequate basis in itself for challenging India's policy of non-alignment. Moreover, even though in 1977 accusations of pro-Soviet bias came not just from the West but also from the Janata Party as it campaigned against Mrs Gandhi in the March elections, the Janata government, when in power, rapidly made clear that the fundamental strength of India's links with the Soviet Union would not be challenged.

In any case the ideology of non-alignment has been of far less concern to India, whether in the United Nations or the Non-Aligned Movement itself, than the practical implications of the resolutions adopted and the political stance of member states which may follow from such resolutions. In this sense India's participation has been conditional on the acceptance of its determination to protect its regional interests. Where necessary it has made concessions of tact but not of substance to its partners in the NAM.

This is well illustrated by India's failure to invite Heng Samrin's government of Kampuchea to the NAM summit in New Delhi in 1983. One of Mrs Gandhi's first acts on regaining office in January 1980 was to recognize Kampuchea's Vietnam-sponsored government. Given India's friendship with the Soviet Union and hostility to China such recognition was hardly surprising, though it was naturally unpopular with many South-East Asian states. Recognizing that some leaders would not attend the New Delhi summit if the Heng Samrin government were invited, Mrs Gandhi left it off the invitation list. At other times India has not hesitated to deflect the thrust of UN or NAM resolutions or to ignore them when it seemed in its interests to do so, though it has preferred to try to prevent such embarrassments. Two issues which have a direct bearing on India's security illustrate this point: India's attitude to nuclear non-proliferation and its stance on the Indian Ocean as a Zone of Peace proposals.

Nuclear non-proliferation

Despite consistent pressure from the West and from the Soviet Union to sign the Nuclear Non-Proliferation Treaty, India has steadfastly refused to do so. Through the late 1970s and the 1980s the New Delhi government pressed the view that India could not consider signing until the major powers demonstrated their own commitment to disarmament. It has refused to obey the rules of what it regards as a club organized by the 'haves', which is trying to impose rules on the 'have-nots', irrespective of the interests of those states which have not yet qualified for membership.

President Carter gave up his attempts to use the exports of uranium for the Tarapur reactor as a bargaining counter to persuade India to sign the NPT immediately after the Soviet occupation of Afghanistan. His pressure had been deeply resented in India, but the President gave three reasons to Congress for his change of mind and going ahead with the shipment: first, American foreign policy objectives in the region would not be best served by such pressure; second, 'the cut off of fuel would put at risk existing safeguards at Tarapur and its spent fuel, and possibly hasten India's venture into recycling as an alternative source of fuel', thereby representing an even greater threat to non-proliferation; and third, legal grounds.[6]

The Indian government has argued that China's actual nuclear capability and now Pakistan's imminent potential are major threats to its own security, and it regards keeping the nuclear option open as vital to its security interests. Thus when the United Nations adopted Resolution 3265B on 9 December 1974 (just seven months after India's underground nuclear explosion in Rajasthan), proposing that South Asia be declared a nuclear-free zone, India's reluctance to see the proposal furthered contributed to its remaining a dead letter.

Resisting American pressure to sign the NPT was always less difficult and embarrassing for India than rejecting similar Soviet urging. Highly placed officials in the Indian government recognize that in the post-Afghanistan period, and in the context of proven superpower reductions in nuclear weaponry, Soviet pressure under President Gorbachev is going to be stepped up significantly. When Gorbachev met Rajiv Gandhi in December 1988 in New Delhi he extended a pressing invitation to sign the Treaty. Although he took it no further when the Indian prime minister made it clear that he was not going to do so, those present were in no doubt that it would be re-issued with increasing insistence. If relations with China improve and Pakistan also shows a willingness to halt its nuclear programme, that pressure will become more difficult to resist.

The Zone of Peace

With the proposal to designate the Indian Ocean as a 'zone of peace' (the IOZOP) – a concept first mentioned in Cairo in 1964, then seriously advanced at the NAM summit in Lusaka in September 1970 and subsequently endorsed by the United Nations in Resolution 2832 – India hoped to eliminate the superpower military presence from the Indian Ocean. However, Sri Lanka, one of the original proposers of the motion, refused to go along with India's wish to specify the United States base on Diego Garcia without reference to all military bases in the Indian Ocean.

This debate has remained a feature of discussions on the Zone of Peace proposals throughout the 1980s. For its part, India was concerned that the proposal might be used by its neighbours in the region, especially Pakistan, to restrict its own developing naval influence in the Indian Ocean, which through the 1970s and 1980s it has seen increasingly as a vital part of its security zone. In justification for this fear, India pointed to Pakistan's attempt to introduce an amendment to the 1981 resolution tabled at the Ministerial Conference of the NAM in February 1981, by which the Ocean and all littoral states would be declared nuclear-free. Rajan has argued, however, that this was more a placatory move made in the context of the debate between India and Sri Lanka than an attempt to restrict India's defensive options.[7]

The failure to make substantial progress on implementing the IOZOP concept was not just the result of the unwillingness of the superpowers, especially the United States, to participate, but also of the fact that the littoral states did not all share the same goals. India's position was ambiguous, not so much because of its emphasis on removing the American naval presence, as because of its concern to build up its own naval presence to a level commensurate with its perceived regional power requirements. However defensive that growing capability may be, it is a capability that some of India's neighbours fear and do not wish to be excluded from consideration in the IOZOP proposals.

At the same time India's support for demilitarizing the Indian Ocean struck a sour note in Indo-US relations. A Congress team that visited South Asia in 1981 remarked acidly on India's condemnation of the US naval base on Diego Garcia while 'pointedly failing to comment on the Soviet occupation of Afghanistan', and Western powers have resented India's reluctance to acknowledge any legitimate interests in the Indian Ocean region other than their own.

The United Nations and the Commonwealth

Economic matters have become increasingly important for India in the United Nations and the Non-Aligned Movement. India has played a highly active part in UNCTAD, the UN Conference on Trade and Development. UNCTAD's triennial conferences have repeatedly been dogged by the unwillingness of the developed world to make anything like the concessions to Third World trade hoped for by those in the developing world. The global recession in the early 1980s, coupled with the sharp rise in oil prices, stimulated renewed efforts to tackle economic problems not only in UNCTAD but through the Non-Aligned Movement.

In practice there is little scope for immediate direct cooperative action between member states of the NAM. Not only are the majority of their economies small and weak, they have little mutual complementarity. From 1980 onwards, many of them were saddled with crippling debt burdens, a problem which, as has been shown in Chapter 4, India was largely spared. However, India has added its very significant weight to arguments from the non-aligned for a reform of the world's monetary system and for measures to tackle debt, stressing particularly the importance of understanding the interdependency of the world's economic order.

The Commonwealth offers India multinational cooperation on a quite different footing from that established by the United Nations or the Non-Aligned Movement. While in theory at least the UN is universalist, the Commonwealth links countries with a measure of common history and extensive political, economic and cultural ties. The bilateral links between Britain and India, which declined sharply up to the early 1970s but which remain important, have inevitably changed in substance and in relative significance. As for the Commonwealth, after some apparent initial hesitation on Nehru's part as to whether India should join at all, successive Indian governments have valued the opportunities for informal contacts with countries from diverse social and economic backgrounds.

This is not to say that India, any more than other members of the Commonwealth, sees it as a vehicle for the making or implementation of high policy. Few in India would disagree with Professor Dennis Austin's verdict that 'the fact that the Commonwealth has moved away from the high noon of its post-war confidence to a more sober judgment of its worth does not necessarily spell extinction ... There may be room ... among the Commonwealth's governments for argument not only as a means to understanding but as the clearing ground for agreement.'[8]

Certainly the Janata government of 1977–9 made great play of being much more actively pro-Commonwealth than Mrs Gandhi's government had been. Morarji Desai joined forces with Australia's then prime minister, Malcolm Fraser, to launch Commonwealth Heads of Government Regional Meetings in 1977. Then in 1989 Rajiv Gandhi was quick to offer to sponsor Pakistan's re-application for membership of the Commonwealth, in the wake of its return to democracy. Such a move may have had an added piquancy in the light of the Commonwealth's refusals to re-admit Pakistan under President Zia ul Haq's leadership, and doubtless the opportunity for India to be seen to be openly burying the hatchet was welcome positive publicity. But it would be wrong to underestimate the sincerity of the gesture.

By far the most difficult problem has been the handling of South Africa's apartheid policy. India has strongly attacked apartheid ever since Independence, and as mentioned above it was the first subject raised by India in the United Nations. India played a major part in the decision taken at the Heads of Government Meeting to establish an Eminent Persons Working Group on the question of sanctions against South Africa, and was represented on the group by former Minister Swaran Singh. Between 1987 and 1989 he served on the eight-country Commonwealth Foreign Ministers Committee on Southern Africa.

The decision of Britain to stand out against an otherwise unanimous report was greeted with widespread dismay in India, and Britain's continued isolation on the issue of South Africa at the Vancouver Commonwealth Heads of Government Meeting in 1987 proved a further frustration. An additional reason for sensitivity on this issue is not just the presence of over three-quarters of a million settlers in South Africa of Indian origin, although that plays an important part. Equally, educated public opinion is sensitive to the difficulties faced by Indian immigrants in Britain, which have been widely reported in the Indian press. Such stories often carry a theme of British racial prejudice towards Indians, and Britain's reluctance to impose sanctions on South Africa is widely interpreted as casting doubt on British professions of belief in multiracial equality. Ironically, as Peter Lyon has suggested, to many Indians the Commonwealth link is still seen basically in terms of a link with Britain, however anachronistic this view actually is today.

India's extra-regional bilateral ties

India's membership of multilateral institutions has played a major part in its diplomatic activity, but its foreign policy outside the South Asian region has not been restricted to such forums. Bilateral relations with states with which India has common interests have played a vital part in the country's foreign policy initiatives. It has been particularly active in securing its interests in the Middle East. Political reasons for this stance were paramount up to 1971, but since then the economic boom in the Gulf states and the associated opportunities for employment for Indians have introduced significant economic and social reasons for the development of friendly relations.

The oil price rises of 1973 and 1980 also made it imperative for India to explore new markets. Just before the overthrow of the Shah, it entered into ambitious programmes of economic cooperation with Iran which were designed to enable India to pay for its increased oil imports with the export of engineering goods, cement, sugar and iron ore among a range of other goods. Although the Iran-Iraq war prevented many of the anticipated trading links from materializing, India is still doing everything possible to maintain good relationships with the new regime.

In India's foreign relations in West Asia political considerations have remained to the fore. Protection of its security interests vis-à-vis Pakistan have given urgency to the need to sustain good relationships with Iran and Iraq as well as Saudi Arabia. Over the forty years since Independence there has been little reason for India to change its pro-Arab rather than pro-Israeli policies. It is possible that, as some members of the Israeli lobby in the United States are arguing, the prospect of a Pakistani nuclear bomb and its possible spread to other countries in the Islamic world may give India and Israel a common interest that up to now has not existed. Even with that incentive it is unlikely that India's fundamental platform of friendship with the Muslim world will be shaken.

India's economic links with much of Africa are slight, India's exports to Africa accounting for only 2.5% of total exports in 1985–6 compared with 8.4% in 1970–1. The contrast with trade with the rest of Asia is striking. Exports to Asia rose from Rs 1.7 billion in 1970–1 to Rs 13.1 billion in 1985–6. Imports rose even more dramatically, from Rs 0.5 billion to Rs 24 billion in the same period. Those figures show that by 1986 the other countries of Asia were exporting more to India than either the United States or the Soviet Union and nearly twice as much as the United Kingdom. This growing economic interest, notably for inward investment, is greatly strengthening ties with Japan in particular, which is beginning to show real interest in India, as well as other parts of Asia, as a home for investment.

India and the United Kingdom

The special nature of India's links with the United Kingdom has undergone an inevitable transformation in form and content since 1947, but they remain more significant than the purely economic interrelationship might suggest. In 1975 Lipton and Firn analysed what they termed the erosion of the relationship between Britain and India, a process which gathered pace particularly rapidly between 1960 and 1970. Despite that erosion, the link with Britain remains of much greater significance than that between India and any other middle-power country.

Despite the common historic links and the continuing mutual interests in economic cooperation, India's relationship with Britain since 1971 has followed a bumpy road. The fierce criticism of British immigration policy in the late 1960s and 1970s has given way to keeping a close eye on the treatment of Indian immigrants in Britain. There is wide understanding over Britain's framework of legislation to restrict immigration, and a recognition that large-scale emigration from India is not only totally unrealistic but would also do nothing to help tackle India's domestic problems. However, there has been great disquiet over the treatment of immigrants in Britain. Travellers to the United Kingdom have also been subject to what has widely been seen as harassment and demeaning tests at points of entry. The strength of this feeling has brought about attempts by the British government both to explain policy and to mitigate the damage done to relations between the countries.

Yet the most serious cause of Indian unease in the relationship with the United Kingdom has been that of Sikh terrorism in the Punjab. Some reliable sources suggest that there are members of the Indian government who believe, fanciful though it doubtless appears in the United Kingdom, that the British government has tolerated the sending of money and arms, as well as political support, for Sikh extremists and terrorists based in the United Kingdom as a means of applying political pressure on the Indian government. However, both the failure to agree an extradition treaty such as that which was successfully negotiated with Canada, and the accompanying disputes, caused serious disquiet. Nevertheless, by the end of the 1980s that fear had largely subsided.

Alongside these problems the substantial economic activity of the twenty years since 1971 has not simply been a continuation of the colonial relationship. Since 1971 the rapid weakening of the economic ties that had characterized the 1960s as a delayed response to the end of the colonial links has been halted. In 1985 over 47% of foreign-owned industrial assets in India were still British-owned. British capital also had a controlling interest in by far the largest number of foreign companies which had Indian subsidiaries, managing assets of over Rs 12 billion. This compared with Rs 4 billion for the United States and Rs 2.4 billion for West Germany.

However, while the figures suggest that the decline of British interest evident in the 1960s had been slowed, the overall relative importance of British investment in the Indian economy continued to decrease over the last two decades. Furthermore Britain's large relative share of foreign-owned assets was mainly a legacy of the past. Its share of new foreign collaborations, at only Rs 230 million between 1981 and 1986, was much smaller than that of not only the United States and West Germany but Japan and even non-resident Indians.

As we have seen in Chapter 4, the relative importance of Britain as a trading partner also diminished, for although absolute values of trade between Britain and India increased in real terms between 1971 and 1988, Britain's share in India's trade continued to decline, albeit at a slower rate than in the 1960s. Such a relative decline is not simply the result of a post-colonial malaise. Rather, it demonstrates the widening range of India's economic interests and its increasingly active pursuit of international collaborators in development.

Much of this activity has come from the private sector, but the Indian government under Rajiv Gandhi has moved to reduce the barriers to inward investment. In the period 1970–80 Indian collaborations with Europe 'were concentrated in sectors that are technology-intensive by international standards'.[9] An EC/India report on technology transfer and investment found that the overwhelming majority of agreements were made in response to Indian demand, largely driven by the rapid growth of the engineering industry in India and its search for high technology. The scale of increase in such agreements, and in joint ventures generally, is striking, and the European Community countries are major beneficiaries. The United Kingdom has lagged behind West Germany in such investment, and in the early 1980s was third overall after the United States and the FRG. As was shown in Chapter 4, however, other European countries have been increasing their interaction with India more rapidly, and along with Japan promise to reduce still further the relative significance of the United Kingdom as a source of private capital.

This may in part reflect a relative reluctance on the part of British industry to enter into joint ventures in comparison with that of other countries. The British government itself has been noted in India more for encouraging India to consider large-scale government-to-government investment, sometimes under the aid budget. To some highly placed Indian businessmen such an emphasis is misdirected. Some of the aid deals, such as the virtual gift of Westland helicopters in 1987, attracted extremely adverse publicity, though in late 1989 the Indian government was negotiating a further order.

As Bell and Scott-Kemmis report, among the major objectives of Indian government policy in the 1960s and early 1970s were: '1. minimising the price paid for the technology itself . . . 2. reducing the extent to which equipment and components were tied to technology imports . . . 3. reducing the number of agreements entered into.' By the 1980s increased emphasis was being given to 'issues about the technological dynamism of Indian industry'.

One of the most striking results of research in the mid-1980s was the finding that approximately fifty per cent of British firms which entered into collaborative agreements with Indian companies regarded the results as 'unsatisfactory' – a far higher proportion than was found with West German companies. Bell and Scott-Kemmis reported that 'failure seemed to be associated with inadequate efforts on the part of British firms to evaluate prospective projects, to estimate the costs involved in transferring the technology required for effective operations in India, or to make provision for unforeseen eventualities.'[10]

For their part, some British and other European firms regard India as a difficult country in which to work. Such difficulties are attributed largely to the administrative procedures which it was necessary to work through during the 1970s and 1980s if joint ventures were to be established successfully. Licensing policy was one of the major economic targets of Rajiv Gandhi's first period in office. The strong vested interest of India's bureaucracy, coupled with the ideology of central planning, was commonly blamed for the slowness in bringing down the barriers to an increasingly competitive economic environment. However, there are strong business interests also on the side of a highly protectionist policy, and any Indian leader will have to show determination to see through changes on the scale that V.P. Singh initiated in his 1985 budget.

India, the USA and the Soviet Union: geostrategic interests

South Asia borders on, but is not in itself, a region of primary geostrategic interest for both the United States and the Soviet Union. Chubin suggests that 'US relations with India have never been of sustained or overriding importance to the US in the post-War era. They have in practice been the subject of sporadic and derivative interest, the sum of tactical expedients rather than overall design.'[11]

Superficially this might appear strange. Much proclaimed as the world's largest democracy, recently released from an imperial past, with a culture having nothing in common with atheistic Marxism and having the potential for developing one of the world's largest markets, India might have seemed a natural area of intense American interest. Yet there were only comparatively short periods before 1971 when Indo-American relationships prospered. Ironically, by far the most striking friendly American act towards India was its decision to send it arms in 1962, to assist in the war with China. The popular response to that gesture of friendship was remarkable, symbolized by the images of President Kennedy which suddenly found a prominent place on tea-shop walls across India among the faded photos of Nehru, Gandhi and Subhas Chandra Bose, and gaudy icons of Krishna, Lakshmi, Ganesh and other gods of the Hindu pantheon. But despite that, and the very large quantities of American aid that flowed to India through the 1960s, it was not long before the photos came down. Twenty years later it would be difficult to imagine the photograph of another American president in their place, which had by then been taken by that of a different charismatic president, Mikhail Gorbachev.

Zbigniew Brzezinski's autobiographical account of his years as President Carter's National Security Adviser is very revealing.[12] In 587 pages, India receives a total of seven passing mentions, six being the one word 'India' in lists of other names. In contrast, China is the subject of over 70 pages of analysis. Perhaps even more strikingly, in his 'fifty key policy recommendations for the US government in the 1990s', listed at the end of *Game Plan*, India is not mentioned once.[13]

The relatively peripheral role played by India in American thinking is overstated by such indicators, but there is no doubt that since 1971 India has figured more prominently as an irritant to successive US administrations than as a major country with which the United States has strong common interests. 'The long term goodwill between the US and India results from US support for Indian independence, US economic assistance to India, and the bond created by our open, democratic societies. The growing Indian immigrant community in the US, estimated now at some 600,000, is making notable contributions to American society and also provides a human link to India.'[14] Optimistic views of Indian-US relations such as these in *Gist* are commonly expressed in highly generalized terms. In contrast, day-to-day relations have frequently been characterized by mutual suspicion, distrust and sometimes outright hostility.

The Nixon-Kissinger initiative towards China in 1971–2 worsened relations with India. According to Raju Thomas the transformation of American thinking, and the consequent enhanced Indian fear of China, may have helped to push India towards the Indo-Soviet Treaty of Friendship in 1971.[15] Alternatively it could be argued that Indian fears at that time were focused more on the dangers of a Soviet-Pakistani alliance or even detente, which would have militated severely against Indian interests. The Soviet Union had advanced the offer of a friendship treaty to India at least as early as 1969, but Mrs Gandhi was only moved to take it up in the middle of 1971, partly under the enormous pressure of 10 million refugees from East Pakistan crowded on to Indian soil.

Nevertheless Henry Kissinger himself viewed the Indo-Soviet Friendship Treaty as a clear move away from India's stance of non-alignment. When the secessionist movement in Bangladesh became a war between India and Pakistan, the United States strongly condemned what it saw as India's determination to break up Pakistan. It feared not only Indian domination of the subcontinent but the extension thereby of Soviet influence. In any event, India had nothing by way of comparable geopolitical significance to offer the United States, which by 1971 had already embarked irrevocably on its new policy towards China. At the same time its South Asian policy of supporting Pakistan as a counterbalance to potential Indian regional dominance was on the point of collapse. Its decision to send the fleet into the Bay of Bengal in December 1971 not only deeply and fruitlessly antagonized Indian public opinion: it threatened direct superpower military confrontation. Pran Chopra suggests that on 11 December 1971, one day before the US force reached the Bay of Bengal, the Indian government was promised Soviet support in the event of US attack,[16] although according to one eyewitness account in the Indian prime minister's office, no one was apparently more relieved that it failed to materialize than the Soviet ambassador. The prestige the Soviet Union had already gained through the signing of the Friendship Treaty was being put on the line unexpectedly and embarrassingly early. To have had it tested by military action was the last thing the Soviet Union wanted.

Rudolph and Rudolph suggest that 'the nadir for United States cultural policy and programs was probably reached in 1971, when US Government policies and actions alienated Indian, Pakistan and Bangladesh governments and public opinion.'[17] After 1971 Indian-US relations have fluctuated with unpredictable speed from moments of euphoria through to uncomprehending mutual distrust.

Mrs Gandhi's opposition to American involvement in Vietnam, her support for Hanoi, and her repeated claims that the United States was involved in efforts to destabilize her government, made relations in the early 1970s particularly difficult. When Patrick Moynihan was US ambassador to India (1973–5) he reportedly 'pressed the Embassy to find out just what the United States had been up to.' He relates in his memoirs, published in 1978:

> I was satisfied we had been up to very little. We had twice, but only twice, interfered in Indian politics to the extent of providing money to a political party... Both times the money was given to the Congress Party, which had asked for it. Once it was given to Mrs Gandhi herself, who was then a party official. Still, as we were no longer giving money to her, it was understandable that she should wonder just to whom we were giving it.[18]

Although India showed an interest in diversifying its source of arms supply by seeking new deals with the United States in 1974, the uncertainties of the relationship were symbolized by the cancellation of a scheduled visit to New Delhi by President Ford in April 1975.

Mrs Gandhi's domestic political problems, culminating in the declaration of a state of emergency in 1975, saw her receive effusive backing from the Soviet leadership, which was still extremely anxious over the developing American-Chinese link and concerned to protect as far as possible its South Asian flank. The ousting of Mrs Gandhi by the new Janata government in March 1977, following closely on the election of President Carter in the United States, saw hopes rise both in India and in the United States that relations would improve. The new Indian foreign minister, Atal Behari Vajpayee, said on 30 September 1977, for example, that 'there is undoubtedly a feeling in India that the United States under President Carter pulsates today with a new idealism and inspiration. Both in India and the United States there is a new confidence that the cynics can be overwhelmed by the idealists.'

Certainly President Carter and his new administration went out of their way to make new overtures to India, according it a renewed priority in the region as potentially a major power. The decision to block the sale of A-7 aircraft to Pakistan can be seen in this light. But deeper problems of identifying exactly where American interests in India lay remained unresolved.

Weiner, for example, criticized the unwillingness of the superpowers to take South Asian regional issues seriously in their own terms rather than projecting on to them their own global concerns.[19] As an argument in favour of US involvement in South Asia, he pointed to India's potential power adversely to affect US interests in the region. Others have also argued that there are positive benefits to be obtained from cultivating a much more positive relationship with South Asia and with India in particular.

India's explosion of a nuclear device in 1974 was evidence of its ability to interfere with America's perceived global interest in nuclear non-proliferation. In the late 1970s a major stumbling-block to permanently improved relations was the question of India's use of heavy water for the Tarapur reactor.

While this disagreement slowed progress towards building a more trusting relationship, it also rapidly became evident that the new Janata government would remain on close terms with the Soviet

101

Union. The Soviet government eased this process by rapidly switching its support to the new Janata regime, an exchange of visits between Soviet and Indian leaders cementing the mutual recognition of continuing common interest. This served to strengthen Indian stereotypes of the comparative value of relations with the United States and the Soviet Union: on the one hand, the United States was regarded as at the same time patronizing, arrogant and unreliable as a partner, and on the other the Soviet Union was seen as eager to maintain friendship come what might.

The end of the Janata regime at the close of 1979 coincided with the Soviet occupation of Afghanistan. From the return of the Congress Party to government in January 1980 the two superpowers have played a crucial role in influencing India's foreign policy and its relations with its neighbours. A deep unease was felt by many in the Indian government over the Soviet Union's presence in Afghanistan, which made it not just an Asian power but a South Asian power. Such disquiet was exacerbated by fear over the American rearming of Pakistan.

The occupation of Afghanistan forced a radical review by the American administration of its South Asian strategic interests and of some of its key policies. Most strikingly, the effective moratorium on arms sales to Pakistan was reversed. In 1978 the then recent cancellation of the sale of A-7 aircraft to Pakistan had reinforced the evidence of the previous decade that 'in the Department of State and the White House, at least, ... there is a preference ... for an intraregional political solution to the security concerns of India and Pakistan. This policy seems to be based on the reality that arms transfers to either India or Pakistan will be resented by the other, and a general disinclination to contribute to military competition in the region.'[20] Throughout the 1980s Indira Gandhi and then Rajiv Gandhi pressed the American government to recognize the dangers of the regional arms race.

The Reagan administration reinforced the Carter administration's policy. Although Carter's offer of $400 million of military aid had been spurned as 'peanuts' by President Zia ul Haq, who argued specifically that the aid was not enough to compensate for the risks of identifying with US policy in the region,[21] the Reagan administration determined that its major interest lay in supporting Pakistan to the hilt. In the view of Selig Harrison, 'to politically conscious

Indians the prospect of some form of American help for Pakistan in the event of another conflict is not far-fetched. This underlying distrust of American intentions is the most important of several critical factors that are converging in the Indian Ocean-Persian Gulf region to create new dangers as well as new opportunities for American diplomacy.'[22]

India's interests in the Soviet occupation of Afghanistan did not lie simply in the arrival of Soviet power on their regional doorstep. Within Afghanistan itself the Indian government was deeply concerned at the spread of fundamentalist Islam. The possibility that an extremist Islamic government could take over in Kabul continues to excite very real Indian anxiety. Not surprisingly, India deeply fears the implications for American policy in the region of conclusions such as those of Brzezinski, for what he terms the 'soft underbelly' of the Soviet Union: '1. Washington should work to reinforce the resilience against Soviet advances by providing more aid to Pakistan and by being willing to improve relations with Iran. 2. The United States should keep the Afghan issue alive by sustaining the resistance, while simultaneously probing for Soviet willingness to restore genuine neutrality and internal self-determination.'[23]

Despite the increasing evidence of the breakdown of the US and Western-backed alliance of Afghan Mujahidin which comprised the so-called interim government, American support for the war continued into 1990. According to one report, the CIA was 'taking over more direct management of arms distribution and military strategy for the mujahidin from the Pakistan army'.[24] While Brzezinski had long returned to academic life, his doctrine appeared to live on.

When such goals are explicitly allied to the objective of keeping the 'Indo-Soviet axis' under control, Brzezinski is simply echoing a policy enunciated by Richard Nixon on a visit to Delhi in 1953 as Vice-President. Harrison records how 'explaining the projected American decision to provide military aid to Pakistan, Nixon observed that it would, among other things, "help to keep Nehru in line" '.[25] In the current period of superpower detente the reiteration of such sentiments seems strikingly anachronistic.

Despite the inevitable damage that the renewal of arms supplies did to US-Indian diplomatic ties, there were periods of increased optimism as to the potential for a constructive relationship. Mrs Gandhi made a highly successful visit to the United States in 1982.

But by 1984, when she was asked if she was satisfied with the state of US-Indian relations she replied bluntly 'not really'.[26] She had been particularly concerned by the drastic reduction in soft loan funds made available for development through the IDA, and the US, policy of arms supply to Pakistan. The United States, for its part, remained unhappy at India's 'refusal to oppose more forcefully the Soviet occupation of Afghanistan'.[27]

By the mid-1980s, with the election of Rajiv Gandhi's government in India, voices were once again being heard in the United States urging that India be taken seriously as a focus of long-term American interests. In June 1985 Rajiv Gandhi made arguably the most successful official visit by any Indian leader to that country. Francine Frankel wrote : 'The time has come for Washington to develop a policy that views New Delhi as more than a minor player in the global superpower competition or simply one of dozens of Third World or non-aligned countries.'[28]

But how were common interests between India and the United States perceived? Stephen Cohen, giving evidence to a Congressional committee in May 1985, suggested: 'I don't think we can treat South Asia on an intermittent basis. The disasters of the past, and I would include Afghanistan, have been due to American forgetfulness in South Asia ... government operations should flow from policy and policy should be based on interests, but rarely have I seen this actually occur in American policy towards South Asia.'

Cohen went on to acknowledge that there were perhaps no vital US interests in India, but at least five important ones: support of South Asian countries against Chinese and Soviet threats; common democratic value systems; the large-scale movement of skilled and professional Indians to the United States; the smuggling of narcotics and opium-derived drugs into the United States from Pakistan; and finally, the possibility of nuclear proliferation in South Asia. To those could surely be added the movement of oil through the Indian Ocean. At the time the Soviet Union occupied Afghanistan more than half the world's seaborne oil was carried on Indian Ocean routes – 14 million barrels a day to Europe and the United States, 3.7 million barrels a day to Japan and the east.[29]

The Memorandum of Understanding (MOU) initialled in May 1985 suggested there were grounds for the new optimism. Rajiv Gandhi, speaking to the US Congress, claimed that 'the peoples of India and America are not allies in security strategies, but they are friends in larger causes – freedom, justice and peace.'[30] On 17 October 1986, speaking in Auckland, Rajiv Gandhi said US-Indian relations had registered a 'tremendous improvement'.[31] There were hopes that India was now in a position of strength vis-à-vis the United States and that this would induce better relations with Pakistan, Sri Lanka and China.[32]

Yet once again the apparent promise has been slow in delivering substantial improvements. The MOU was only very slowly implemented, with particular delays in the transfer of sensitive high-technology exports to India. However, it has not prevented important positive developments from taking place. The United States accounted for the second largest share of investment by foreign companies in the 1980s. Investment from the United States for collaboration with Indian companies rose from Rs 22.5 million in 1981 to Rs 294 million in 1986, and while this is still a tiny proportion of its total investment abroad it outstripped that from any other country. The difficult negotiations which finally resulted in Pepsi-Cola winning the right to re-enter India in 1989 as a major food processor, initially for export, testify to the continuing political sensitivity of large-scale US economic involvement in India. While that sensitivity shows no sign of diminishing, there is evidence that the new American administration under President Bush is taking a far more positive view of India's importance in Asia than did the Reagan administration. There is no doubt that both countries could benefit greatly, economically and politically, from an improved relationship.

The Soviet hand of friendship

Between 1971 and 1986 the Indo-Soviet relationship blossomed from one based on a limited perception of mutual strategic interest to the most enduring and trusting friendship enjoyed by the Soviet Union with any country outside the Soviet bloc. In 1978 India secured Soviet oil for the first time, and during the 1980s oil exports from the Soviet Union rose sharply to account for nearly 70% of exports to India by 1985, while machinery accounted for only 15%. In exchange India exported agricultural products including cereals, raw materials and consumer goods to the Soviet Union. Despite problems over barter trading arrangements, with India reluctant to buy 'obsolete technology', Indo-Soviet trade increased fivefold between 1975 and 1985. The Soviet Union has encouraged India to buy nuclear reactors and finally, after years of pressure, India agreed in May 1988 to buy two Soviet pressurized water nuclear reactors as part of its plans to have 10,000 MW nuclear capacity by the year 2000.

Then Gorbachev's visit in November 1986 was one of the most flatteringly dramatic demonstrations of India's importance in Russian eyes that could have been imagined. Accompanied by a 110-strong delegation of the most powerful members of the Soviet government, he not only established an excellent personal rapport with Rajiv Gandhi, but promised a massive new injection of economic and military assistance.

Yet the very scale of the visit and the exuberance of the propaganda display only highlighted the questions that were beginning to rise in Indian minds. As Peter Duncan has perceptively argued, 'on occasions when Moscow feared a loss of influence in New Delhi – as happened over signs of improving Sino-Indian relations, and after the invasion of Afghanistan – the Politburo made a particular effort to offer Soviet goods to India, evidence that the Soviet leaders were prepared to pay an economic price to maintain their influence.'[33] Certainly significant mutual economic and security benefits had flowed from the Indo-Soviet Treaty of Friendship. But following the Soviet leader's Vladivostok speech in 1986, fears began to grow in India that the new Soviet warmth towards China might spell weaker links with India. Gorbachev's reluctance, in response to questioning from the Indian press, to promise direct military support for India in the event of a possible conflict with Pakistan or China was in line with his commitment to his new emphasis on international cooperation and the peaceful resolution of disputes.

The message was encapsulated in the Delhi Declaration on Principles for a Nuclear-Weapon-Free and Non-Violent World, signed on 27 November 1986 and claimed by both sides as a triumph of the new diplomacy. But the message of 'friendship with all' was read in some Indian circles as 'and a weaker relationship with us'. Thus when Gorbachev visited India again as President in December 1988 he was reported as showing some pique 'at unfriendly speculation suggesting that the ardour of the Indo-Soviet embrace had cooled considerably'.[34] However, he conformed to the long-standing Soviet pattern of reinforcing his message of continuing friendship with a major economic package. Indeed, in the indisputably changing global political climate, it seems that the Soviet Union may be deliberately switching its emphasis to a more dominantly economic link. It offered the largest ever credit (of 3.2 billion roubles) to back assistance for nuclear and thermal power, space, science and technology development, and civil aviation and petrochemicals. Despite the tinge of uncertainty in the air, there can be little doubt that the Soviet commitment to India will remain strong, and will be strongly reciprocated. The National Front government of V.P. Singh has shown no sign of wanting to downgrade a relationship which still promises assurances of stability, political support and economic assistance in a region where mutual interests may be subject to subtle shifts but remain profound. The key to that relationship now, however, lies far more in the fundamental changes which have already transformed the Soviet Union than in India itself.

After Afghanistan: prospects

Throughout the 1980s India's relationship with the United States was coloured by an undercurrent of fear, fear not so much of direct US intervention in the South Asian region as of the indirect effects of its support for its regional allies, especially Pakistan. The withdrawal of Soviet troops from Afghanistan could have opened the door to a transformation of the relationship between India and the United States. As the Soviet threat to the region is perceived to be reduced, so Pakistan's ability to obtain further transfers of high-technology military equipment will have to be balanced against the risks of seeing both Pakistan and India develop an overt nuclear defence capability.

Both the United States and the Soviet Union undoubtedly see it as strongly to their advantage to limit nuclear proliferation. The United States may well see itself as in a stronger position to exercise leverage over Pakistan now that the Soviet military presence on Pakistan's borders has been withdrawn. Equally, global superpower detente has increased the Soviet Union's leverage with India.

At the same time important common political interests between India and the United States, which at present go almost entirely unnoticed, could be allowed recognition. Thus although American ties to the Gulf diminished dramatically during the 1980s, the OECD countries as a whole have a strong interest in the maintenance of free waterways from the Gulf region and the Indian

Ocean. It is difficult to see what benefit the West would see in the spread of Islamic fundamentalism. Both India and the West, as well as common friends such as Saudi Arabia, are concerned to maintain the wider stability of the West Asian region and to limit the power of fundamentalist movements.

There was little evidence that the Reagan administration recognized the potential of developing policies to match such common interests. Now, however, the reported view of American thinking may well be that the regime of President Gorbachev cannot last and that the USSR should be encouraged down the path of internal fragmentation. This would be speeded by the Islamic movement of its southern provinces. Ahmad Rashid suggested, for example, in August 1989 that 'US intelligence is anxious for a pliant government in Kabul because of the strategic implications of the expected long-term unrest in Muslim Soviet central Asia. The CIA logic is that Mr Gorbachev will definitely fail, the Soviet empire will then start to fall apart, and given lack of access through Iran the US should be positioned somewhere on the fragile underbelly of the Soviet Union.'[35]

The negative views of India in the United States, only partially overcome by Rajiv Gandhi's Washington visit of 1985, may prevent any rapid rapprochement. However, the death of President Zia and the election of a democratic government under Benazir Bhutto may encourage the United States to examine closely its relationship with the new government and its wider strategy.

It is a strategy which has vital implications for India as well as for the region as a whole. The National Front government of V.P. Singh has yet to clarify its own strategy for facing the new regional and global challenges of the 1990s. Like its predecessors, it seems bound to devote much of its energies to coping with domestic tasks as a top priority. In tackling those tasks there is little to suggest that it will make any radical departure from established principles, but the pragmatism that has been a hallmark of its relationships with the superpowers is likely to remain a dominant motif.

7
CONCLUSION

India: an aspiring great power?

In 1990, twenty years after India's own turning-point, the whole international political and economic system has itself reached a critical juncture. The erosion of the certainties of the bipolar world is having a fundamental impact upon regional relations in different parts of the globe. The effect on South Asia may well be profound. There, the US-Soviet rivalry, particularly after the Soviet intervention in Afghanistan, exacerbated the tensions which have plagued Indo-Pakistan relations since Independence. As was argued in Chapter 5, the South Asian subcontinent has remained economically as well as politically divided. Such division has left India the major regional power in South Asia. Do the changes taking place now within the country itself and in the wider world suggest that India may emerge as a power of much greater global significance?

To Nehru India already had the makings of a world power when it attained independence in 1947. In Nehru's terms that power was based not on the projection of military might across the region or the globe, but on its potential to provide leadership in the search for an escape from war and poverty. But India's ability to provide that leadership was in constant danger of being compromised, on the one hand by the difficulties of developing national integration and on the other by the threat of external attack. India's foreign policy after 1971 was founded on the same basic premises that Nehru put forward at Independence, but the general principles he laid down were substantially fleshed out and given shape. In relation to India's recent experiences, plans and capabilities, underlying the commitment to non-alignment and peaceful coexistence was a determination to protect India's political, social and economic interests.

After the promise of the 1950s, the 1960s had turned into a decade of near-despair for India. Economic failure, the creaking performance of its ambitious planning system, military humiliation at the hands of China, inconclusive wars against Pakistan, and the political instability surrounding the search for a replacement for Jawaharlal Nehru, had left searing marks on India's still weakly developed sense of national identity. Talk both of moral leadership and of great power status seemed increasingly unreal. Still anxious to preserve its independent integrity, India felt in need of powerful friends.

Thus at the end of the 1960s domestic and global factors pushed India and the Soviet Union onto a convergent course. After a very chilly early relationship the past twenty years saw their friendship blossom. To many in the West this friendship was difficult to understand. Yet the benefits of the relationship were clearly mutual. The Soviet Union went to great lengths to consolidate its friendship with India. In addition to its structural support for the economy and for the armed services it secured friends in positions of political influence. However, it would be a mistake to attribute Soviet ties with India simply to the Soviet perspective. In 1971 India's need for friends was particularly acute. The Indo-Chinese war of 1962 and the wars with Pakistan in 1965 had pointed up the two major threats to India's security. Throughout the 1960s, as relations between the Soviet Union and China turned from warm friendship to frigid hostility, the geopolitical basis was laid for Indo-Soviet friendship. In India's case it was enhanced by China's new friendship with the United States and by Pakistan's growing links with China.

By 1971 that triangular relationship had set alarm bells ringing in New Delhi. The Indo-Soviet Friendship Treaty was the result. To Indira Gandhi this gave the advantages of additional support without the disadvantages of explicitly compromising non-alignment. India did not seek an alliance with the Soviet Union, and although it did buy large quantities of arms on highly preferential terms, it firmly resisted all Soviet pressure to join any collective security pacts. The treaty and its subsequent developments offered substantial mutual economic benefits. The barter trade that was established, despite India's difficulty in the mid-1980s in finding Soviet goods that it really wanted in exchange for its own, had positive aspects for both parties. With both economies at a roughly equivalent level of technology, Indian manufactured goods could be exported to the Soviet Union along with primary products.

But it was enhanced political and military security that was the Friendship Treaty's chief attraction. For the Soviet Union, India provided a strong and stable friendship which was particularly important while relations with China were so bad.

By 1990 India's economic and security situation seems to bear little resemblance to the picture presented twenty years earlier. Economic growth and military expansion, coupled with the break-up of Pakistan, have lent India an air of regional supremacy. There can be no doubt that the peace, stability and development of the whole South Asian region in the immediate future depends crucially on the way in which India itself develops. As the world's second largest country, with a growing economy and the world's third largest standing army, it is already a regional and extra-regional force to be reckoned with. Within the next twenty years it could become one of the biggest markets in the world, with an active sphere of influence stretching across the Indian Ocean as far as the littoral states of both west and east. Its central location within South Asia and the Indian Ocean region, coupled with its size and increasing pace of development, place it in an increasingly important geostrategic position in an emerging multipolar world. If a vacuum is created within East and South-East Asia by the withdrawal of the superpowers, is India now preparing to step into that gap, contending with China for a far wider regional supremacy?

The evidence of the previous chapters suggests that the chief concerns of India's foreign policy after 1971 were focused not on the projection of its power across an ever-widening region but on defensive attempts to protect its own fundamental security interests. After all, where and how would a militaristic India, such as is conjured up by the image of an aspiring world power, project and exercise its military might? Would a dramatically expanded blue-water navy be used to protect supposed Indian interests on the African or South-East Asian or even Australasian littorals? Would the development of missile technology and nuclear weapons be used as a means of extracting territorial concessions from China? To pose the questions is also to answer them.

In a world where old superpower relationships are becoming increasingly irrelevant, the nature of world power status is itself undergoing radical change. Many of the domestic challenges that faced Jawaharlal Nehru remain to be resolved in India today. Despite its economic progress, there were many more millions of desperately poor people in India when Rajiv Gandhi left office than when his grandfather died. Equally, while national integration has made remarkable progress, regional, ethnic and religious tensions continue to pose threatening challenges to internal stability and security. Thus while India has continued to react to immediate events relating to its vital interests since 1971, it now faces the need to re-examine its longer-term objectives and strategies. New possibilities for a constructive relationship between India and Pakistan following Pakistan's return to democratic government still seemed alive at the end of 1989. Rajiv Gandhi's initiative towards reconciliation with China suggested that the new detente could spread further and when it took power V.P. Singh's National Front government was intent on trying to continue and even speed up the process of regional detente.

In its relations with its neighbours India has sometimes acted with the gangling awkwardness of the overgrown youth, unaware of his own strength when surrounded by much smaller children. The characterization of India as a regional bully is misplaced, but during the 1980s it often showed little awareness of the difficulties its much smaller neighbours face in relationships with what to them is a dominant power.

Yet the democratic stability and increasing prosperity of India is essential for the much wider region of which it is the hub. It is also a country with which the European Community and the Western world share not only democratic traditions but a widening range of economic interests. Along with its partners in Europe, Britain could play an active part in fostering links with the India of tomorrow rather than treasuring memories of the India of yesterday. There could be a great deal of mutual benefit to be gained from a new freshness in the relationship.

To many in the West it was a surprise and a disappointment that India failed to take sides openly against the Soviet Union after the invasion of Afghanistan. It would have been far more surprising had it done so. Although relations both with Britain and with the United

States remained important, neither enjoyed the geostrategic position of influence over Indian interests that was held by the Soviet Union. Furthermore, in India British interests were seen as being almost deliberately reduced during the 1960s. New investment from Britain had declined in the post-colonial period, and by 1971 Britain had dropped enough hints that it no longer saw India as a priority region of influence for India to believe that British friendship and support were no longer reliable.

In the 1980s those hints multiplied. While the need for tough immigration laws was widely accepted, Indian immigrants in Britain, unlike those in the United States, were often seen to be having a comparatively hard time. Britain's aid to India declined along with its aid to other parts of the world, fees for overseas students were raised dramatically, a black financial cloud hung over the highly valued work of the British Council, and for a time even the voice of British democratic culture, the BBC World Service, seemed threatened. Old links were decaying but the opportunity of building new links to replace the old had not been fully seized. As an Indian diplomat in Britain candidly observed, 'Britain and India have no real conflicts of interest, but each has the capacity to irritate the other.'

That capacity to irritate was evidenced in multilateral forums too. Indian positions on a number of issues in the late 1970s and early 1980s (the Soviet occupation of Afghanistan and the US bombing raid on Libya are just two examples) were seen in some British quarters as opposed to Britain's interests. In fact for far too long the relationship has been clouded by a false sense of nostalgic sentimentality, stronger perhaps on the British than on the Indian side. This produced an atmosphere which has inhibited understanding of the real and extensive degree of common interest not just between India and Britain but between India and the wider Western world.

At present there are four major areas of common interest between India and the West. The first is economic development. British business is often very conscious of the difficulties of working in India, whereas it is seemingly less aware of both the short-term and the longer-term benefits. The fact that between 1970–1 and 1985–6 India's imports from Japan rose twice as fast as those from Britain suggest that Japan was taking a far more dynamic approach to the Indian market. India's significant development since 1971 and changing economic policies are beginning to effect changes in the economic climate which will demand to be taken seriously by Britain if it is not to lose still more of its industrial share.

The second common interest of India and the West is the importance of peace and stability in the Gulf. Domestic political interests and the importance of oil have combined to keep India's relationships with the Muslim world in the forefront of its thinking since 1971. As Selig Harrison has argued, to Western eyes India has shown too little appreciation of the legitimate security interests of the United States and Western Europe in the Gulf region and of its need to maintain naval forces to protect those interests. Yet the Iran-Iraq war demonstrated the fundamental unity of interest of all oil-dependent states in securing the long-term peace of the region. It is a unity of interest that has yet to be adequately expressed in political action.

A third mutual interest might be held to lie in the containment of Islamic fundamentalism, though this did not appear to be a priority for either the American or the British governments during the 1980s. Continued support for the Afghan Mujahidin suggested that Islamic fundamentalism was still seen in some Western governments as a better protection against communism than supporting moves for a political settlement. In the Indian view such support could prove very short-sighted. Religious extremism is a threat not only to the peace of the Middle East but also to India's own security. This is not just in the form of Islamic fundamentalism but also in the various politicized forms that religious fundamentalism has taken since 1971. There is scope for greater cooperative effort between India and the West in understanding the roots of fundamentalist movements and in strengthening democratic institutions where they exist.

The fourth and last, but not the least, of the immediate shared interests is restricting the spread of nuclear weapons. The West has never been sufficiently willing to understand India's resistance to signing the Nuclear Non-Proliferation Treaty. In China it already had a hostile neighbour with nuclear arms. With Pakistan on the nuclear threshold, there is the risk that political pressures in India will make a nuclear arms race on the subcontinent inevitable.

Two factors present a brief opportunity to prevent that race. On the one hand the withdrawal of Soviet troops from Afghanistan makes it possible for the United States to re-examine its posture towards the whole South Asian region. Given full international support, there is no fundamental reason why the common interest of India and Pakistan to develop peaceful cooperation should not become a reality. Britain and the Western alliance should do far more to foster it.

India has now absorbed its Nehru legacy and is poised to move on. Yet essential features of the foreign policy that Nehru himself developed seem set to remain central to the new government's foreign policy thinking. The pragmatism which has underlain India's foreign policy throughout its independent history does not look threatened. Maintenance of India's national integrity, a continued push for rapid economic development, and the protection of national security interests are the themes which dictated the main thrust of India's foreign policy between 1947 and 1971. The reality of global detente provides a context within which regional detente could also grow. This would relax India's nervousness about neighbouring states exploiting ethnic tensions inside India, and would encourage greater cooperation in many fields.

The political and economic benefits which would flow from seizing that opportunity would be enormous. Within its region there is great economic potential which could be released first by regional detente and then by active bilateral and multilateral cooperation. India could give a lead in breaking away from the negative stalemate with Pakistan, actively seeking areas, notably in sharing the control and use of the waters of the Punjab system, where cooperation could bring both immediate and long-term benefits. On a wide range of issues where economic development and ecological protection are intertwined, cooperation between the nation states of South Asia could bring benefits unobtainable to the states acting independently. Chapter 5 showed the remarkably low degree of economic integration of the South Asian region. If political detente were to lead to an enhanced role for SAARC, and if the countries in the region were able to increase their economic integration and generate more rapid development, then all should benefit. But India, as the largest economic power, stands to benefit the most. And as the region as a whole became more prosperous, this would strengthen India's voice on a global level.

On a wider front, as the Soviet Union and China become more preoccupied with their domestic political and economic problems, India could strengthen its claims to champion the interests of the developing world. Nearly forty-five years of democratic experience in one of the world's most diverse and problematic societies have given India a collective knowledge which offers it unrivalled opportunities to exercise the kind of leadership in cooperation of which Nehru dreamed. The costs of failing to meet that challenge are daunting. Regional separatist movements threaten not only India but Pakistan and Sri Lanka as well. Some in India may see a short-term party political advantage in sustaining a confrontational attitude to its neighbours. However, the longer-term costs would be devastating. While the rest of the world rapidly develops networks of regional cooperation and economic integration, South Asia would be locked in destructive spirals of rising military expenditure and diminishing economic performance.

Prime Minister Singh undoubtedly shares something of the Gandhian vision of India's future: a strong, secular, generous and tolerant society, basing its foreign policy firmly in the tradition of the Panchsheel. The question is whether the sharply conflicting political forces evident in India today have produced a parliament which can deliver the stable and progressive majority to enable him to fulfil that ambition.

NOTES

Chapter 1

1 J.W. Mellor, *India: A Rising Middle Power* (Boulder, CO: Westview Press, 1979).

Chapter 2

1 J.E. Schwartzberg illustrates this point very effectively in his superb *Historical Atlas of South Asia* (Chicago: Chicago University Press, 1978), Plates III (A,B,C,D); IV (1,2,3); V (1,2,3,4); VI (A 1–3); VII (A 1,2; B 1).

2 A. H. Syed, *Pakistan*, in *World Survey*, No. 76 (London: The Atlantic Education Trust, 1975), p. 10; D.C. Jha, 'The basic foundations and determinants of Pakistan's foreign policy', in K. Arif (ed.), *Pakistan's Foreign Policy: Indian Perspectives*, (Lahore: Vanguard Books, 1986), pp. 12–13; A. Appadorai and M.S. Rajan, *India's Foreign Policy and Relations* (New Delhi: South Asian, 1985), p. 17.

3 *The Independent*, 15 April 1989.

4 R.L. Hardgrave and S.A. Kochanek, *India: Government and Politics in a Developing Nation* (San Diego: Harcourt Brace Jovanovich, 4th edition, 1986), p. 339.

5 L.E. Rose in F. Robinson (ed.), *Cambridge Encyclopedia of India, Pakistan, Bangladesh and Sri Lanka* (Cambridge: CUP, 1989), p. 244.

6 M. Tully and S. Jacob, *Amritsar: Mrs Gandhi's Last Battle*, (London: Cape, 1985).

7 The International Bank for Reconstruction and Development, *World Development Report* (Washington, DC: IBRD, 1988), pp. 224–5.

8 The 1981 Census of India gave India's urban population as 159 million (excluding Assam). The annual rate of urban growth is estimated at

3.9% for 1980–5, suggesting an annual increase in the urban population of over 6 million. United Nations, 'The prospects of world urbanization, revised as of 1984–85' (New York: United Nations, 1987).

9 Quoted in *India Today*, 15 August 1988.

10 This view is well documented by Peter J.S. Duncan in *The Soviet Union and India* (London: Routledge for the Royal Institute of International Affairs, 1989).

11 M. Lipton and J. Firn, *The Erosion of a Relationship: India and Britain since 1960* (Oxford: OUP for the RIIA, 1975), p. 9.

12 S. Chawla, *The Foreign Relations of India* in *Comparative Foreign Relations* series, edited by D.O. Wilkinson and L. Scheinman (Encino, CA: Dickenson Publishing Co., 1976), p. 102.

13 M. Lipton and J. Toye, 'Does aid work in India? A country study of the impact of official development assistance' (forthcoming, 1990).

14 Heimsath and Mansingh, for example, put the figure in the mid-1960s at between four and five million, while they quote the *Statesman Overseas Weekly* for 17 December 1966 as putting the figure at over eight million. C.H. Heimsath and S. Mansingh, *A Diplomatic History of Modern India* (Bombay: Allied Publishers, 1971), p. 333.

15 The former is quoted by H. Tinker, *The Banyan Tree: Overseas Emigrants from India, Pakistan and Bangladesh* (Oxford: OUP, 1977), while the second is taken from the US Department of State, Bureau of Public Affairs, July 1987. It is difficult to believe that the difference is accounted for simply by Indian immigration in the intervening period.

16 A. Lemon and N. Pollock, *Studies in Overseas Settlement and Population* (London: Longman, 1980).

17 Heimsath and Mansingh, op. cit., p. 302.

18 Dulles is quoted in Chawla, op. cit., p. 91.

19 *The Independent*, 15 April 1989.

20 K. Subramanyam, 'India and the Soviet Union' in B.R. Nanda (ed.), *India's Foreign Policy: The Nehru Years* (Delhi: Vikas, 1976), p. 113.

21 J. Nehru, *India's Foreign Policy: Selected Speeches 1946–61* (Delhi: Ministry of Information and Broadcasting, 1961).

22 R.H. Jenkins, 'The Architect of Modern India', *The Observer*, 29 January 1989.

23 M. Brecher, *Nehru: A Political Biography* (Oxford: OUP, 1959), p. 565, quoted in J. Bandyopadhyaya (ed.), *Nehru and Non-alignment in Indian Foreign Policy: The Nehru Years* (New Delhi, Vikas, 1976), p. 171.

24 *The Independent*, 4 February 1989.

25 Some maintain that these were Chairman Mao's Five Principles. They were first enunciated internationally in the Sino-Indian Treaty of 1954, which was concerned with trade and transit through Tibet.

26 The list has become something of a mantra: Nepal 1950, Goa 1961, East

Pakistan 1971, Sikkim 1974, Sri Lanka 1971 and 1987–9, the Maldives 1988, Nepal again in 1988–9.

27 R.G.C. Thomas, *Indian Security Policy* (Princeton, NJ: Princeton UP, 1986), p. 16.

28 R.L. Hardgrave, *India Under Pressure* (Boulder, CO: Westview Press, 1984), p. 136.

29 Subramanyam, op. cit., p. 103.

30 R. Litwak in T. George et al., *India and the Great Powers* (Aldershot, Hants: Gower for the International Institute for Strategic Studies, 1984), p. 115.

31 See for example Appadorai and Rajan, op. cit. (above, Note 2), p. 18, where they point out that India's policy towards Israel as well as towards the Arab states was significantly influenced by this geostrategic influence.

32 Z. Brzezinski, *Game Plan: A Geostrategic Framework for the Conduct of the US-Soviet Contest* (New York: The Atlantic Monthly Press, 1986), p. 3.

33 G.W. Chowdhury records how the Soviet press reacted to Independence in India and Pakistan, describing Nehru's government as 'an Indian variant of bourgeois pseudo-democracy', and Nehru himself as a 'running dog of imperialism'. *India, Pakistan, Bangladesh and the Major Powers: Politics of a Divided Subcontinent* (New York: The Free Press, 1975), p. 8.

34 Chawla, op. cit., p. 95.

35 Rose in Robinson (ed.), op. cit. (above, Note 5), p. 244.

36 Litwak in George et al., op. cit., pp. 142–3.

Chapter 3

1 W.A. Wilcox, *Pakistan: The Consolidation of a Nation* (New York: Columbia University Press, 1963), p. 8.

2 P. Lyon, *India and a Post-colonial State and some other Characterizations* (forthcoming, 1990).

3 The term, meaning 'children of God', was given by Gandhi to the outcastes as part of his efforts to bring dignity to the most despised of India's peoples.

4 *India Today*, 31 July 1988, p. 33.

5 Heimsath and Mansingh argued that in 1960–1 India tolerated forces opposed to King Mahendra; 'propaganda, subversion and outright raids against the Nepali government were launched or appeared to come from India by dissident Nepali factions, while the Indian government appeared to be unaware that flagrant breaches of international law were thereby being perpetrated'. C.H. Heimsath and S. Mansingh, *A*

Diplomatic History of Modern India (Bombay: Oxford University Press, 1971), p. 212.

6 P.R. Brass in F. Robinson (ed.), *Cambridge Encyclopedia of India, Pakistan, Bangladesh and Sri Lanka* (Cambridge: CUP, 1989), p. 188.

7 A very senior member of the Bangladesh government confirmed privately to me in 1986 that his government never took Mrs Gandhi's pledge seriously.

8 M. Weiner, *Sons of the Soil: Ethnicity and Political Conflict in India* (Princeton, NJ: Princeton UP, 1977).

9 *India Today*, 30 June 1989, p. 9.

10 L.I. Rudolph and S.H. Rudolph, *The Regional Imperative: US Foreign Policy towards South Asian States* (New Delhi: Concept, 1981), p. 15.

11 C.P. Schleicher and J.S. Bains, in R.W. Gregg (ed.), *The Administration of Indian Foreign Policy through the United Nations* (New York: Oceana Publications, 1969), p. 34.

12 N. Jetly, *India-China Relations 1947–77* (New Delhi: Reliant Publishers, 1979), p. 2.

13 P. Lyon, The foreign policy of Rajiv Gandhi's Raj, p. 15. Unpublished paper presented to the Royal Institute of International Affairs, 25 January 1989.

14 Brass in Robinson (ed.), op. cit., p. 177.

15 ibid., p. 183.

16 R.P. Cronin, 'South Asia: current developments and issues for U.S. policy', Congressional Research Service Report No. 86–741F, 19 June 1986, p. 13.

17 *India Today*, 31 May 1988, p. 72.

Chapter 4

1 R. K. Sharma, for example, claims that 'Indo-Soviet co-operation has helped to place India among the top ten industrial nations of the world'. R.K. Sharma, *The Economics of Soviet Assistance to India* (New Delhi: Allied Publishers, 1981), p. 2.

2 George Blyn, *Agricultural Trends in India, 1891–1947: Output, Availability and Productivity* (Philadelphia and London: Pennsylvania UP and OUP, 1966).

3 M. Lipton et al., 'Planning the Improvement of Planning in India and Pakistan', supplementary paper in M. Faber and D. Seers (eds.), *The Crisis in Planning* (London: Chatto and Windus, 1972, vol. 2), p. 68.

4 A. Appadorai, *The Domestic Roots of India's Foreign Policy 1947–1972* (Delhi: Oxford University Press, 1981), p. 87.

5 Government of India, *Economic Survey 1988–89* (New Delhi), p. 28, Table 1.21B, and p. 31, Table 3.4.

6 *The Tata Statistical Outline of India 1988–89* (Bombay: Tata Services, Department of Economics and Statistics, 1987), Table 59, p. 64.

7 P.J.S. Duncan, *The Soviet Union and India* (London: Routledge for the RIIA, 1989), pp. 78–9.

8 *India Today*, 30 June 1989, reported on both the cost overruns and the technical failings of the plant. According to a report in *The Independent*, 1 August 1989, India's nuclear plants are the least efficient in the world, narrowly behind those of the United Kingdom.

9 These figures are taken from the *Tata Statistical Outline of India 1988–89* (op. cit., above, Note 6), Tables 52 and 56.

10 Duncan, op. cit., p. 69. He makes the further point that 'Indians themselves have noted that whereas American aid was directed mainly towards consumption, Soviet aid was intended to increase production'.

11 Numerous Indian publications paint Soviet aid in glowing colours. See, for example, Sharma, op. cit., pp. 3–4.

12 Unless otherwise stated the aid figures quoted in US$ are taken from from the IBRD's *World Development Report, 1988* (Oxford: OUP, 1988). Figures quoted in rupees are taken from the Government of India's *Economic Survey 1988–89*. It should be noted that the figures on aid given by the *Economic Survey* are commonly significantly higher than those given by the Reserve Bank of India, which are used in numerous other reference texts, such as the Confederation of Engineering Industry's annual *Handbook of Statistics*, or the *Tata Statistical Outline of India*, p. 150.

13 Only the People's Republic of China, Afghanistan and Kampuchea, among the low income countries, received less (*World Development Report, 1988*, Table 22, p. 264).

14 M. Lipton and J. Toye, *Does Aid Work in India? A Country Study of the Impact of Official Development Assistance* (forthcoming, 1990).

15 ibid., p. 31.

16 Quoted in Appadorai, op. cit., p. 100.

17 *Current* (Bombay), 16 May 1987, p. 12.

18 *Economic Survey 1988–89*, Table 7.4, pp. S 84–5.

19 Duncan, op. cit., p. 73.

20 *Confederation of Engineering Industry Handbook of Statistics 1988* (New Delhi: Confederation of Engineering Industry, 1989) p. x.

21 *Economic Survey 1988–89*, Table 6.7, p. S-72.

22 *Economic Survey 1988–89*, Table 6.9, p. S-76.

23 Confederation of Engineering Industry, op. cit., p. xii.

24 Duncan, op. cit., pp. 74–7.

25 These data come from the *Pakistan Yearbook 1986–87* (Islamabad: Government of Pakistan, 1986).

26 *Economic Survey 1988–89*.

27 *India Today* (New Delhi: Living Media India, 1985), p. 61.

28 Confederation of Engineering Industry, op. cit., Table 17.5.

29 'New singer, old song', *Far Eastern Economic Review*, 4 January 1990, pp. 50–2.

30 *SIPRI Annual Survey of Military Expenditure, Arms Trade and Conflicts* (Oxford: OUP, annual series).

31 Duncan, op. cit., p. 79.

Chapter 5

1 L. E. Rose, in F. Robinson (ed.), *Cambridge Encyclopedia of India, Pakistan, Bangladesh and Sri Lanka* (Cambridge: CUP, 1989), p. 236.

2 Lawrence Ziring, 'Bhutto's Foreign Policy, 1972–73' in J.H. Korson (ed.), *Contemporary Problems of Pakistan*. Quoted by B. H. Farmer, *An Introduction to South Asia* (London: Methuen, 1983), p. 114.

3 Quoted by M. Tully and Z. Masani, *From Raj to Rajiv: Forty Years of Independence* (London: BBC Books, 1988), p. 145.

4 Raju G.C. Thomas, *India's Security Policy* (Princeton, NJ: Princeton, 1986), p. 7.

5 The extremely advantageous terms obtained by India for Soviet arms may in part have reflected the warmth of Mrs Gandhi's own relationship with the Soviet leadership. A senior Indian official suggested to me that Mrs Gandhi was on excellent personal terms with both Marshal Ustinov and with Admiral Gorshkov.

6 D. Mukerjee, for example, argued that 'India quietly set aside its own declared policy of excluding superpowers from its region and raised no objection to the Soviet presence beyond the Hindu Kush Mountains, South Asia's traditional defence perimeter'. D. Mukherjee, 'US Weaponry for India', *Asian Survey*, VII, 6, 1987, pp. 595–614.

7 V. P. Dutt, *India's Foreign Policy* (New Delhi: Vikas, 1984), pp. 382–3.

8 'Weapons and Technology', *SIPRI Yearbook 1988* (Oxford: OUP), p. 56.

9 Quoted by V. Longer in *The Defence and Foreign Policies of India* (New Delhi: Sterling, 1988), p. 325.

10 Professor Anirudha Gupta, 'India and the security of South Asia', paper delivered at seminar at the Institute of Commonwealth Studies, London, 24 January 1989.

11 Ashley J. Tellis, 'Aircraft carriers and the Indian Navy', *Journal of Strategic Studies*, vol. 10, no. 2, 1987, pp. 141–67.

12 See Chapter 6 for a fuller discussion of this question.

13 B. H. Farmer, *An Introduction to South Asia*, op. cit. (Note 2 above).

14 Kumari Jayawardena, *Ethnic Conflict in Sri Lanka* (Colombo, 1985).

15 *Current* (Bombay), 16 May 1987, p. 4.

16 Personal communication, May 1987.

17 *India Today*, 30 June 1985. The euphoria was to be shortlived. Bhandari himself retired in March 1986 to be succeeded by A. P. Venkateshwaran, by which time India's Sri Lanka policy was deeply in the mire.

18 *Times of India*, 19 May 1987.

19 ibid., 28 October 1986.

20 *Far Eastern Economic Review Annual Yearbook 1989*.

21 N. Jetly, 'Sino-Indian relations: a quest for normalization', *India Quarterly*, XLII, 1, 1986, p. 54.

22 P. Chawla, *The Foreign Relations of India* (California: Dickenson Publishing Co., 1976), p. 133.

23 D. Woodman, *Himalayan Frontiers: A Political Review of British, Chinese, Indian and Russian Rivalries* (London: Barrie and Rockliff, 1969), p. ix.

24 Alastair Lamb, *The McMahon Line: A Study in the Relations between India, China and Tibet, 1904–1914* (London: Routledge & Kegan Paul, 2 volumes, 1966), p. 232.

25 Farmer, op. cit., p. 137.

26 Jetly, op. cit., p. 55.

27 N. Maxwell, *India's China War* (Harmondsworth: Penguin, 1970), p. 161.

28 Jetly, op. cit., p. 57.

29 ibid., p. 63.

30 *India Today*, 15 May 1987.

31 Jetly, op. cit., p. 62.

32 *Far Eastern Economic Review Annual Yearbook 1989*, p. 185.

Chapter 6

1 A. Appadorai and M. S. Rajan, *India's Foreign Policy and Relations* (New Delhi: South Asian Press, 1985), p. 673.

2 Quoted in M.S. Rajan, *Studies on Non-alignment and the Non-aligned Movement: Theory and Practice* (New Delhi, ABC Publishing House), p. 39.

3 William J. Barnds, *India, Pakistan and the Great Powers* (New York: Praeger for Council on Foreign Relations, 1972), pp. 47–8.

4 P. J. S. Duncan, *The Soviet Union and India* (London: Routledge for the RIIA, 1989).

5 P. M. Kamath, 'Politics and national security: American influence on Indian thinking', *Institute of Defence Studies and Analyses Journal*, vol. 16, January-March 1984, pp. 273–85.

6 US House of Representatives 1981 Committee on Foreign Affairs, 'Congress and Foreign Policy', p. 91.

7 Rajan, op. cit.

8 D. Austin, *The Commonwealth and Britain* (London: Routledge & Kegan Paul for the RIIA, Chatham House Papers No. 41, 1988), pp. 49–50.

9 'Technology transfer and investment'. Report of the EC/India project on problems and perspectives of the transfer of technology between firms in the European Community and India, Berlin, 26–7 November 1984, p. 2.

10 R. M. Bell and D. Scott-Kemmis, *Indo-British Technical Collaboration since the Early 1970s: Change, Diversity and Forgone Opportunities* (University of Sussex: Science Policy Research Unit, 1984), p. 6.

11 T. George, R. Litwak and S. Chubin, *India and the Great Powers* (Aldershot, Hants: Gower for the IISS, 1984), p. 149.

12 Z. Brzezinski, *Power and Principle: Memoirs of the National Security Adviser 1977–1981* (New York: Farrar Strauss Giroux, 1985).

13 Z. Brzezinski, *Game Plan: A Geostrategic Framework for the Conduct of the US-Soviet Contest* (New York: The Atlantic Monthly Press, 1986).

14 *Gist*, July 1987, p. 2.

15 R. C. G. Thomas, *Indian Security Policy* (Princeton, NJ: Princeton University Press, 1986), p. 10.

16 Pran Chopra, *India's Second Liberation* (Delhi: Vikas, 1973), p. 201.

17 L. I. Rudolph and S. H. Rudolph, *The Regional Imperative: US Foreign Policy towards South Asian States* (New Delhi: Concept, 1980), p. 30.

18 Quoted by R. L. Hardgrave and S. A. Kochanek, *India: Government and Politics in a Developing Nation* (San Diego: Harcourt Brace Jovanovich, 4th edition, 1986), p. 289.

19 M. Weiner, 'Critical Choices for India and America' in D. C. Hellmann (ed.), *Southern Asia; The Politics of Poverty and Peace* (Lexington, MA: Lexington Books, 1976), p. 65, quoted by R.P. Cronin, *The United States, India and South Asia: Interests, Trends and Issues for Congressional Concern*, Subcommittee on Asian and Pacific Affairs, Committee on International Relations (Washington, DC: Library of Congress, 1978), p. 9.

20 Cronin, op. cit., p. 41.

21 US House of Representatives 1982 Committee on Foreign Affairs, 'Congress and Foreign Policy', p. 104.

22 Selig Harrison, 'Cut a Regional Deal', *Foreign Policy*, vol. 62, 1986, p. 126.

23 Brzezinski, *Game Plan*, pp. 264–5.

24 *The Independent*, 9 August 1989.

25 S. Harrison, 'Containment and the Soviet Union in Afghanistan', in T. L. Deibel and J. L. Gaddis (eds.), *Containment: Concept and Policy* (Washington, DC: National Defense University Press, 1986, 2 vols.), p. 459.

26 R.P. Cronin, 'South Asia: current developments and issues for U.S. policy', Congressional Research Service Report No. 86–741F, 19 June 1986.

27 ibid.

28 F. Frankel, 'Play the India Card', *Foreign Policy*, vol. 62, 1986, pp. 148–66.

29 R.P. Cronin, *The United States, India and South Asia*, op. cit., p. 11.

30 *India Today*, 15 July 1985, p. 53.

31 *Deccan Herald*, 18 November 1986.

32 B. Sen Gupta, *India Today*, 15 June 1985, p. 60.

33 Duncan, op. cit., p. 112.

34 Dilip Bobb, *India Today*, 15 December 1988, p. 14.

35 A. Rashid, 'Words to stop the killing', *The Independent*, 9 August 1989, p. 17.

FURTHER READING

Asian Survey, India Today and *India Quarterly* carry frequent topical articles on India's politics and foreign relations. Other books not mentioned in the Notes include:

Agarwal, A. (ed.), 1987. *The State of India's Environment*, Second Citizens' Report, New Delhi, Centre for Science and the Environment.

Agwani, M.S., 1976. 'India and the Arab World', pp. 78–102 in B.R. Nanda (ed.), *Indian Foreign Policy: The Nehru Years*, New Delhi, Vikas.

Bhargava, G.S., 1972. *Success or Surrender: The Simla Summit*, New Delhi, Sterling Publishers.

Burki, S.J., 1988. *Pakistan under Bhutto*, 2nd edition, London, Macmillan.

Cassen, R.H., 1978. *India: Population, Economy and Society*, London, Macmillan.

Chaliand, G. and J-P. Rageau (tr. T. Berrett), 1983. *Strategic Atlas: A Comparative Geopolitics of the World's Powers*, New York, Harper & Row.

Clarkson, S., 1979. *The Soviet Theory of Development: India and the Third World in Marxist-Leninist Scholarship*, London, Macmillan.

Diehl, A., 1978. *Periyar: E.V.Ramaswamy*, New Delhi, B.I. Publications.

Frankel, F., 1978. *India's Political Economy, 1947–1977: The Gradual Revolution*, Princeton, Princeton U.P.

Horn, R.C., 1982. *Soviet-Indian Relations: Issues and Influence*, New York, Praeger.

Jha, S.K., 1975. *Uneasy Partners: India and Nepal in the Post-Colonial Era,* New Delhi, Ramakant.

Khoshoo, T.N., 1986. *Environmental Priorities in India and Sustainable Development*, New Delhi, Indian Science Congress Association.

Further reading

Muni, S.D. and A. Muni, 1984. *Regional Co-operation in South Asia*, New Delhi, National Publishing House.

Rajan, M.S., V.S. Mani and C.S.R. Murthy, 1987. *The Nonaligned and the United Nations*, New Delhi, South Asian Publishers.

Sen Gupta, B., 1970. *The Fulcrum of Asia: Relations among China, India, Pakistan and the USSR*, New York, Pegasus.

Sen Gupta, B., 1986. *Regional Co-operation and Development in South Asia*, New Delhi, South Asian Publishers.

Sen Gupta, B., 1983. *Nuclear Weapons: A Policy Option for India?* London, Sage.

Tinker, H., 1976. *Separate and Unequal: India and the Indians*, London, Hurst.